prayers FOR A SIMPLER LIFE

PRAISE FOR PRAYERS FOR A SIMPLER LIFE

"I'm drawn to the simple life. Maybe because as a homeschooling mom of ten and an author, things are rarely simple. Yet no matter how busy our lives are, Faith Sommers reminds us what really matters: hope, trust, and faith that God is with us in things big and small. This is a delightful book that highlights how God's Word applies to everyday life. It was uplifting to my soul!"
—TRICIA GOYER, BESTSELLING AUTHOR OF OVER SIXTY BOOKS, INCLUDING *THE ONE YEAR BOOK OF AMISH PEACE*

"With Scripture, wisdom, prayer, and real-life truths, Faith Sommers shows us the many ways God cares for us. The devotions are short enough to be read in a few minutes, yet deep enough you could spend hours of study and prayer if you want to. This will be a devotional I will likely spend a lot of time in."
—LAURA V. HILTON, AUTHOR OF *THE AMISH FIREFIGHTER*

"Come here to gather your daily manna. You will find strength, hope, peace and will stand in awe of God's grace. No matter her walk in life, every woman can feel a kinship to Faith Sommers as she shares her real-life stories, coupled with God's Word."
—MARIANNE JANTZI, AUTHOR OF *SIMPLE PLEASURES: STORIES FROM MY LIFE AS AN AMISH MOTHER*

"Prayers for a Simpler Life is just plain inspiring! Author Faith Sommers shares her faith and offers encouragement through Scripture, analogies, meditations based on life experiences, and prayers that call the reader into a deeper spiritual life in Christ. This artistically designed book offers thirteen weeks of quiet meditations focusing on who God is, our relationship with him, and how a simple and honest faith affects our daily lives."
—JANICE L. DICK, AUTHOR OF HISTORICAL AND CONTEMPORARY FICTION

prayers FOR A SIMPLER LIFE

*Meditations from the Heart
of a Mennonite Mother*

FAITH SOMMERS

HERALD PRESS

Harrisonburg, Virginia

Herald Press
PO Box 866, Harrisonburg, Virginia 22803
www.HeraldPress.com

Library of Congress Cataloging-in-Publication Data
Names: Sommers, Faith, author.
Title: Prayers for a simpler life : meditations from the heart of a Mennonite
    mother / Faith Sommers.
Description: Harrisonburg, Virginia : Herald Press, [2017]
Identifiers: LCCN 2016040485 | ISBN 9781513801261 (pbk. : alk. paper)
Subjects: LCSH: Mennonite women--Religious life. | Christian life--Prayers
    and devotions. | God (Christianity)--Meditations.
Classification: LCC BX8128.W64 S64 2017 | DDC 242/.643--dc23 LC record avail-
able at https://lccn.loc.gov/2016040485

PRAYERS FOR A SIMPLER LIFE
© 2017 by Herald Press, Harrisonburg, Virginia 22802. All rights reserved.
Library of Congress Control Number: 2016040485
International Standard Book Number: 978-1-5138-0126-1 (paperback);
    978-1-5138-0278-7 (hardcover)
Printed in United States of America

Unless otherwise noted, Scripture text is quoted with permission from the *King
James Version*.

26 25 24 23 22   13 12 11 10 9 8 7 6 5 4

TO MY DEAR HUSBAND, Paul, without whose love and support I would never have attempted this project. I thank God for you and the balance and joy you bring to my world.

TO OUR CHILDREN, Michelle, Carlon, Logan, Hans, Grant, and Charlotte. You have endured hastily cooked meals and an occasionally absentminded mother with patience and humor. I cherish you.

TO MY PARENTS, who encourage me to write, and whose own talents have inspired me. Your support humbles me.

TO MY EXTENDED FAMILY, brothers and sisters, parents-in-law, cousins, aunts, uncles, and to all of you who have touched my life, for you I give thanks.

TO GOD, who deserves my praise, my honor, my awe, and my life. Because of you, I write.

CONTENTS

ACKNOWLEDGEMENTS

I thank my sisters, all of you, sisters by birth and sisters-in-Christ, thank you for your faithful prayers and encouragement. Thank you for letting me use incidents from your lives in this book. Thank you most of all for being examples of what Jesus can do in the lives of those who are truly committed to him.

Special recognition goes to Susan Wheary and Sue Avina. Your gracious and talented editing polished my scribbles. Also a heartfelt thank you to Herald Press editors, Melodie Davis and Valerie Weaver-Zercher. You have been honest, courageous, and extremely helpful. I am indebted.

My father passed away soon after this manuscript was completed. He was excited about it and enjoyed reading the devotionals. His interest and involvement in my writing were great motivators. My life is forever changed by his passing. I will miss his love, support, and words of wisdom. I am deeply indebted, not only for the blessing of his encouragement, but also for the legacy of faith which is my inheritance.

A DAY IN THE LIFE OF THE AUTHOR

The ultimate test of life is the living of it
from day to day. —TAUTOMU FUKUYAMA

The early morning hour is my favorite time of day. I love the quiet moments to pray and read the Bible before my husband wakes the children. The morning rush isn't as stressful as it was when the children were younger, but it still takes organizing to get everyone on their way.

We always have lunches to pack for my husband and sons who work in construction. During the school year we also have school lunches to prepare, which are usually done by the oldest child in school.

On Wednesdays during the last school term, I drove the children to school. We live in a small rural community, and five of us mothers took turns (each chose one day weekly) transporting ten of the twelve students to our little one-room school. Classes are conducted at one end of the church house.

After daily "morning work," which includes sweeping floors and tidying the house, each day of the week holds different duties. We wash laundry and iron clothes on Monday and Thursday; with our dry climate the clothesline gets full duty except on rare rainy days, which occur only during the short winter.

As anyone with a family knows, a schedule is open to interruptions, rearrangement, or exceptions. But our family functions best when we try to follow a plan.

On Tuesdays I often write, sew, or paint. During the school year I am alone at home. Our oldest daughter teaches school in another community, the three older boys work with their dad, and the two younger children attend school.

We sew our own dresses and head coverings. For the men in the house, I only sew suspenders; the rest of their clothes are purchased. We also share clothes with others in the church or extended family. Well-made fabric doesn't easily wear out, so dresses can be handed down for several years. It's a true blessing for a busy mother to receive ready-made clothes.

I have always enjoyed art, and my parents graciously provided an oil-painting class when I was a teenager. What a wonderful gift that was! My whole family reaps the harvest from the seed planted that day. Some of our children also like to draw, and on winter evenings it's not unusual for us to sit around the living room with sketch pads and pencils.

God has also given me a passion for the written word. Books are an essential (come to my house and I will let you choose a book from our library), and so are notebooks and pens. About twenty years ago my husband purchased a writer's course for my birthday (only another writer could understand why that brought joy). It opened a world of blessing and fulfillment. Another thing that has enriched my life and my writings are writers' critique groups. We share tips, edits, and ideas for each other's writing, from a Christian perspective.

On Wednesdays, I might do the shopping, mending, or baking. We bake bread and cookies, grape nuts and granola, cakes and pies. As for the mending pile . . . my sewing machine is always at the ready, but it still seems as though as soon as I think we're caught up, another button pops off a shirt or another knee pushes through a pant leg. Our sons are learning the basic stitches and sometimes they do their own mending. I love to see that.

Two Wednesday evenings a month we have prayer meeting and Bible study at church. One Sunday night a month we have hymn singing. It's a blessed time to sing as we sit around tables. We share a snack and fellowship afterward.

Friday is our main cleaning day, although we vacuum and dust throughout the week. The children help with these tasks. About once a week I drive to a town thirteen miles away for groceries, although sometimes it's less often. My husband generously picks up needed items on his way home from work, as he passes through that little town nearly every day. The larger towns, with shopping malls and big-box stores, are about thirty miles away.

We grow a small garden mostly for fresh eating; with produce and fruit available year-round from local stands or markets, we don't plant as much as we did when we lived in the Midwest. I do can and freeze some vegetables and fruits. Everything takes a great deal of water, as it seldom rains here from May through September.

Saturday is normally a family day to work on projects around the house and in the fields. We have a small orchard, with citrus and other varieties of fruit, and also an acre of young English walnut trees. Chickens, a dog, a cat, and cattle constitute our farm animals.

Since our community is small, we don't have many activities, and our evenings are generally spent as a family. We enjoy an early supper and then play together or work on family projects.

On Sundays, we gather with the members of our small congregation for Sunday school and a sermon preached by one of our three ministers. We have a fellowship dinner one Sunday a month; we bring food and share the noon meal together after the church service. There are about fifty-five people, young and old, in Maranatha Christian Fellowship. We also have a few local attendees most Sundays. Anyone is welcome!

The quote that I put at the heading of this "day in the life" reminds me of a young lady who spent a weekend with us. She needed to study a religion for a college course and chose to interview the Mennonites. After she had been with us for a day, she said, "I had planned to ask you what your religion means to you, but now I realize it's not just a religion—it's your way of life." Praise God. That's what Christianity should be and do!

A MOMENT IN THE MORNING

A moment in the morning, ere the cares of day begin,
Ere the heart's wide door is open for the work to enter in;
Ah, then alone with Jesus, in the silence of the morn,
In heavenly, sweet communion let your duty day be born.
In the quietude that blesses with a prelude of repose,
Let your soul be soothed and softened, as the dew revives the rose.
A moment in the morning, take your Bible in your hand,
And catch a glimpse of glory from the peaceful promised land;
It will linger still before you when you seek the busy mart,
And, like flowers of hope, will blossom into beauty in your heart;
The precious words, like jewels, will glisten all the day,
With a rare, effulgent glory that will brighten all the way.
When comes a sore temptation, and your feet are near a snare,
You may count them like a rosary, and make each one a prayer.
A moment in the morning—a moment, if no more—
Is better than an hour when the trying day is o'er.
'Tis the gentle dew from heaven, the manna for the day;
If you fail to gather early—alas! It melts away.
So, in the blush of morning take the offered hand of love,
And walk in heaven's pathway and the peacefulness thereof.

—Arthur Lewis Tubbs (1867–1946)

1

GOD IS OMNISCIENT

Isaiah 55

*O*ur friend was on an airplane with her young children, heading for their Alaska home from California. A flight attendant struck up a conversation with her. "Oh, you don't want to be on this flight," the attendant said. "This one stops quite a few times before it reaches Anchorage. You want the direct flight." Thanking her, our friends left to switch flights and board the other plane. In Anchorage, her husband was frantic—the first airplane crashed and he thought they were on that flight.

Recently I called someone "by accident." I was returning a call to a number I didn't recognize and reached a friend who needed to talk. After we visited awhile and I shared a few words of encouragement, she thanked me for calling. I thanked God for planning the call.

Does God know the details of each one's life? Does he care? He knows! Despite fog that obscures our vision, God sees everything perfectly. I am mortal, with limited understanding. He is wise, and all knowledge begins with him (Proverbs 1:7).

I can only see the present, with a dim view of the past. It is impossible to know the future, even though I can have a good idea, by studying history, of at least partially where my decisions will lead. Sometimes I wish I knew what the next year will bring. Or even this day.

When I start to fret about a situation and doubt whether I can find my way through, I find peace by recognizing that God knows.

If he is the beginning of knowledge, then learning to know him better should be my daily quest. The best way to gain that knowledge is to study the living words that he gave: the Bible. In honest searching of his Word, I realize that I can rest in the God who knows.

Psalm 44:21: "He knoweth the secrets of the heart."

Psalm 1:6: "The Lord knoweth the way of the righteous."

Job 23:10: "He knoweth the way that I take: when he hath tried me [tested my faith], I shall come forth as gold."

Acts 15:8: "God . . . knoweth the heart."

John 21:17: "Thou knowest all things."

These verses are just a sampling of the many that speak of the omniscience of God. He knows how much I can handle, and he promises to keep me strong. He knows the reason for suffering and trials, even while I cry out in pain and despair. He can see the beginning and the end, and I can only dimly see the present.

When I realize that he is God, and that God knows all about everything, I learn to trust in his grace and seek to obtain his wisdom so that each choice I make will lead me closer to him.

prayer

Dear heavenly Father, you knew all about me before I was born. You know what I will face today, tomorrow, next year. Better than that, you are here, keeping me in your care. I seek to know you better so that your wisdom may guide my choices.

reflection

Are you worried about the future? Today, commit it to the One who knows.

2

GOD IS OMNIPOTENT

Jeremiah 32:16-27

*W*hen my mother was young, she had many ear infections.
Sometimes she grew so ill she would hallucinate. Winters
especially were miserable. As an adult, she was still plagued by ear-
aches. Finally, the doctor decided she needed surgery. It was scheduled, and while they waited, my mother asked to be anointed. This
is taught in James 5:14-16, and even if God chooses not to heal, it
brings peace to the heart.

When Mother arrived at the hospital for the surgery, the doctor
did another test to make sure of the procedure. He was stunned.
Nothing was wrong with Mom's ears! God had healed her!

When one of our friends was dying with cancer, his daughter
said, "It would be such a small thing for God to heal my father."

But in that situation, God healed him by taking him to heaven.
Does that shake my faith in God's omnipotence? In our Scripture
reading, someone asks a poignant question, "Is anything too hard
for the Lord?"

The Bible is full of evidence of God's power. At creation he formed
the world with his words, and he formed human beings with his
touch. Soon after, during the time of Noah, he destroyed nearly
everything that he had made with a worldwide flood, miraculously
sparing Noah and his family, and animals and birds.

During the building of the Tower of Babel (Genesis 11), God created languages and scattered people to all parts of the earth.

In Abraham's lifetime he witnessed many miracles. Prophet Elijah
saw God working in amazing ways (1 Kings 17–19; 2 Kings 1–2).
The Old Testament is full of testimony to God's power.

While Jesus walked on the earth, he performed many miracles.

Was the power only for people in the past? Has God changed? In God's Word, we see: "Jesus Christ the same yesterday, and today, and forever" (Hebrews 13:8).

He has done marvelous things for us. My husband fell twenty-one feet and only a broke his wrist and ankle. Another time he totaled a pickup and survived with scratches. My sons were riding on a trailer that bore a full five-hundred-gallon water tank. Coming up a hill, the tank slid to the right, the opposite of where the boys were standing. Miracles? Absolutely.

Sometimes God lets painful things happen. Death instead of healing. Broken bones instead of safety. Do I still believe that God is all-powerful? Sometimes the miracle is simply a peaceful heart and a trusting mind.

I face daily challenges. Sometimes it is a seemingly insurmountable problem. Can I, even in this situation, believe that God can either change it or help me through it? There is nothing too hard for God.

prayer

Thank you, God, for showing me your awesome power. From day to day, I stand in awe at all you are, at all that you do. May I trust in your power to give me strength for all I will face today.

reflection

Are you facing a mountain that looks uncrossable? In what way can you feel and know God's power to help in this situation?

3

GOD IS OMNIPRESENT

Psalm 139

I was at a grocery store, miles from home. The car would not start, and we had no phone. Aloud, I prayed, "Jesus, please help us." Within minutes, the vehicle was humming. Joyfully, we drove away, singing praises. My three-year-old daughter said, "Mama, is Jesus in the van?" What a great opportunity I had to talk about God and to teach her the song "God Is Everywhere."

As a child, the first time I really thought about the words in that song, I was almost frightened. God is here? Listening to me quarrel with my sisters? Watching me do a sloppy job in my math lesson? Taking note of my attitudes toward an untidy neighbor?

My parents stressed that it should bring comfort—the omnipresence of God. If he is everywhere and I truly believe that, nothing can touch me that doesn't first meet him.

God's omnipresence should bring fear if I am doing wrong, because although God is love, he is also just. The fear of God will keep me aware that he sees, he knows, and he notices everything I say, do, and think. Not only aware, but conscious to consider what I am doing, saying, thinking. Does it glorify God and edify others? If it doesn't do one or both, I should not do it.

When my niece was diagnosed with a brain tumor, my cousin reminded me of this profound truth. She said, "God is here. Even now. Even in this."

In my pain, I reached out and felt his deep concern for my niece and his abiding love for each of us. Truly it brought comfort to know that we were not abandoned by God. Much more, he had my niece in his all-powerful, tender hands. She couldn't be safer anywhere else.

When the surgery was over, the tumor removed, and my niece filled with the vibrancy she had been missing during the year of her illness, we felt overwhelming awe at the mercy of our great God.

The week before the surgery, a dear friend of ours died after a difficult journey with cancer. Wasn't God with him? Why did God choose to heal my niece but take my friend home?

While I know that God is omnipresent, it does not necessarily follow that I understand his ways. Romans 11:33 says that his ways are "past finding out." I need a God like that!

prayer

Dear Father, thank you for being everywhere. Thank you for never leaving me to journey alone. Teach me to live in awe of you so that I do not willfully sin. Keep my heart at peace so that I may find comfort in your presence.

reflection

Does knowing God is everywhere bring you peace or terror?

4

GOD IS ABLE

Ephesians 3

My grandma was dying and requested that all her children come to see her. My mother, living many miles away, didn't know how she could go. My father struggles with ill health, and Mother didn't know if she should leave him or if he was able to travel with her. She prayed and committed it to God. The same day, my brother called Mom. He had purchased an airline ticket for her to fly to see her mother. A sister promised to take care of our father. Mother was able to spend three days at Grandma's bedside. It was a healing, inspiring time for Mom and her siblings. God answered her prayers in ways she had not imagined.

Is there anything that God cannot do? I marvel at verse 20 of today's Scripture. God "is able to do exceeding abundantly above all that we ask or think."

That's amazing. I have imaginations that run wild, I have dreams that surpass reality, I have longings that I know will probably never be realized. Yet God says he can do more, much more, than anything I can imagine.

Do I fear the future? Our children are born into a world that grows increasingly wicked. Will they be faithful? Will they be protected from the evil and the darkness?

I hear of young children with terminal illnesses, and I grow worried when I spot a bruise, a swelling, or hear of an ache. What if I lose this child?

My husband's cousin lost her husband, and she is left to raise a large family. What if something happened to my husband? How would I cope emotionally and financially?

My mind starts whirling. I shudder to visualize the things my family might face. But before I lose my peace, God whispers to my heart. He says, "I am able. I am able to keep them from falling. I am able to watch over them every day, every minute. I am able."

The apostle Paul declared that he knew in whom he believed, and he was persuaded—absolutely convinced—that God could keep all that Paul had committed to him forever, against the day of eternal life.

It reminds me of my friend, who faithfully, determinedly follows God at a time when trusting him is anything but easy. Her sister and mother tend to mock her courage, and her children waver in their faith. But she stands firm because she knows God honors commitment and obedience.

Have I committed my soul unto him? He will keep it for me. Have I committed my faith to him? He will protect it and help it to grow. He is able.

Is there an obstacle I am facing today? God is able to move the mountain, or he may give me strength to climb it.

prayer

Dear God, I thank you that you are able to do much, much more than I can even ask or think. I rest in your power, and as I yield to your will, I know you will work in me what you desire.

reflection

What impossibility is lurking in your life? Commit it to God. Ask to be shown his power.

5

GOD'S AMAZING LOVE

Romans 5:1-8

I cannot remember when I first realized that God loves me. Possibly the first song I learned was "Jesus loves me . . . the Bible tells me so."

I saw God's love in my parents. One of my first memories of my father is kneeling beside him as he prayed by his chair before the rest of the family awoke. In my mind I hear Mother singing as she worked. Always singing of God and how much he loves us.

God created us because he loved us. Our very breath is a token of his love. I think of Adam and Eve, the first humans God created. He loved to walk and talk with them every day.

God still loves to spend time with the people he has created. He loves to talk with me, and if I listen, I can hear his voice. Psalm 19 tells us that he speaks to us by his beautiful world. Even the skies tell of our glorious God.

Because of his love, he moved through humans to write his eternal words for us to follow. On each page of the Bible, his love shines brilliantly.

His love saves. The verses in Romans 5 show that he loved me even while I was a sinner. God didn't have his back turned to me until after I learned to seek, love, and obey him. No, his love is so pure and encompassing that he loves me no matter what I have done.

The greatest act of love was sending his beloved Son, Jesus, to live on the earth as a man and then to die a horribly cruel death for my sins. Jesus was sinless, yet he bore my sins, and when I believe on him and accept him as Lord of my life, I am saved. Amazing love!

His love redeems (Galatians 3:13). Redemption is deliverance from sin through Christ, who paid the ultimate sacrifice, giving his blood. Through redemption, I am restored to a relationship with God that was broken when I sinned.

His love shelters. Psalm 91 talks of how he keeps me safe day by day. And all because he loves me. I am unworthy of his love, but he does not count that against me. He just keeps loving.

The last verses in Ephesians 3 ask me to comprehend how great is God's love. I try desperately to wrap my mind around his love, how great, how wide, how deep, how trustworthy. Finally, I fall on my knees in awe. I can only love him back with all the intensity I find within. Because I love him, I trust him. I obey his Word. That is how I express my love to him.

prayer

Lord, I cannot understand why you love me, but I am so thankful you do. Without your love, my soul would die. I love you, Lord, for giving me life. Physical life, yes, but especially eternal life through the blood of Jesus. With all my heart, I adore and worship you.

reflection

Consider what God is doing for you this week that shows his love. Thank him!

6

GOD IS FAITHFUL AND JUST

1 John 1

Long ago a young man joined the Mennonite church. His life was marked by hardships and loneliness. His first marriage didn't last long—his young wife left him while he was in the military. The second marriage ended when he realized he should not have remarried after divorce (Mark 10). His wife agreed but later married his best friend. He never spoke of his war experiences, or of his hurts. But he faithfully served God with all his heart. He died last year of pancreatic cancer. At the funeral, hundreds of people came to show their respect and love of him, our brother in Christ. He showed clearly God's faithfulness in the life of someone totally committed to God.

God is just. He is fair. Sometimes we say that life isn't fair. Certainly our brother's life didn't seem fair. Perhaps it was not, but God is fair. I cannot see the plan God is working to fulfill, but I can trust him to do all things well.

Even in his justness, God forgives. If I was punished according to my sins, my soul would be in danger of hell and my life would be in ruins. But he forgives when I sincerely repent and confess.

I might be tempted to retaliate when I am wronged. I have thought, "Oh, wouldn't vengeance be sweet?" But it isn't my place to strike back with words or acts of retribution. Romans 12:19 tells us that vengeance belongs to God.

Matthew 5:38-48 speaks clearly of the new law that Christ came to establish. Under the old law, or covenant, people were permitted to hit back. The "eye for an eye" doctrine prevailed. But Jesus says that not only should we not kill, but we should not even think unkindly.

His justice demands my love and loyalty, first of all to him. Love for God motivates love for all humankind. First John 3:10 says that if I don't love my brother (which simply means anyone and everyone), I am not of God. I am not a Christ follower. If I am cleansed from unrighteousness and filled with God's love, I will love others.

Unfortunately, I have already yielded to the temptation to give a hasty, vengeful retort. But revenge is not sweet. It hurts me and it damages relationships. By God's grace, I am learning to let go of the desire to get even. It is not my right. My right is to obey the dictates of the Holy Spirit, who rules in love and righteousness.

God is faithful. I can safely trust him every day, all my life. His faithfulness is an anchor in a changing world. It is a constant no matter what is happening around me.

God's work in my life is faithful. He doesn't get tired of my feeble attempts, my three steps forward, two steps back. He lovingly keeps leading me closer to him, closer to his heart. In his faithfulness, I feel secure. Psalm 119:75 sums it up so well: "I know, O Lord, that thy judgments are right, and that thou in thy faithfulness hast afflicted me."

His justice longs to see me walking in truth so that I may be with him eternally. That's why he, in faithfulness, convicts me of sin and gently leads me back to him.

prayer

Dear God, your faithfulness reaches to the heavens and brings peace to my heart. I trust you. Your justice is right and good. I know you will take care of every detail of my life.

reflection

Can you look back and think of ways God has showed you his faithfulness? How can you be more faithful to him?

7

GOD IS GOOD

Lamentations 3:22-33

*H*ow glad I am that God is good. A few years ago, I was convicted at how easily I said "God is good" when something went well. When I nearly had an accident, when my son's wrist wasn't broken in a fall, when my father's heart surgery was successful, my first thought was, "God is good."

Isn't God good when things go wrong? Last spring, I didn't see a red light and hit a car; another son's wrist was broken in a freak collision at school; my uncle passed away at a young age from a lung disease. Could I still say, genuinely, that God is good?

God's goodness is not measured by the good things that come into my life. The good things do outnumber the bad, and I gratefully count my blessings. Yet, even in the setbacks, the disappointments, the sorrows, I know that God is good.

A friend has come through severe emotional distress. She was adopted and often felt unloved and unaccepted. When she was a young girl her family was robbed, and the resulting fear dogged her life. Eventually she became physically ill to the point of death. Still she longed after God. In his mercy, he led her to a doctor and to a program of restoration. While she wishes healing were instant, she recognizes even in the daily struggle to trust him that God is good. She has been given tools to work through the hurts of the past. She knows God loves her personally, and she joyfully shares a testimony of his grace. Her face shines with his goodness.

Life isn't always easy. This is a fallen world, where pain and death are part of life. I have only to glance at the headlines in the daily paper to be reminded how much I need God's abiding presence.

Romans 8:28 is a comfort and an encouragement to me when I wonder why something happened. "And we know that all things work together for good to them that love God, to them who are the called according to his purpose." Opening my heart to receive him will also open my life to the good he longs to work within me.

Psalm 145:9 tells me, "The Lord is good to all." There are many verses that speak of the goodness of God. Romans 2:4 chides me, reminding me that it is the goodness of God that leads me to repentance. Because of his goodness and his love, he wants me to experience his forgiveness and cleansing.

When I struggle to understand, if I seek his face, by prayer and reading his Word, he brings peace and courage that I desperately need. That is because they are the words of life, words of truth, words of promise from a God who is good.

prayer

Dear heavenly Father, thank you for being good and for blessing my life with good. Even when bad things happen, I know that you are good and you do good. I cling to you and pray that you will continue to perform in me that which is good, for your glory.

reflection

Are you facing a painful experience? Look around you; find reasons to praise God for his goodness, even in the pain.

1

STRESSED OUT OR BLOOMED OUT?

2 Corinthians 4:6-18

*M*y African violet had finally bloomed! I was thrilled with the velvety blooms, and a bit awed. That a plant would bloom so profusely for me—the lady with the not-so-green thumb—seemed like a miracle.

In a year or so the pot was full of tiny violet sprouts encircling the mother plant. Surely I could do the proper gardening thing and transplant them. We would then have five violet plants to enjoy.

To my disappointment, a veteran gardener informed me that violets bloom most vigorously when they are root-bound. Unless I was willing to wait perhaps another year for the newly transplanted violets to blossom, I would have to keep my one plant as it was.

It was a difficult choice. I did eventually divide the plants, but it was true—it was quite a while until any of them bloomed, even the original hardy violet. It took patience and years of growth.

More recently I heard that plants under stress will also bloom, whereas they might not if coddled. The analogy was thought-provoking. I would like my life to be pain free, stress free, and always pleasant. But that's not life. And it's not good for me.

My cousin lost a baby, and during the time of grief, her spirit shone with God's grace. While not everyone can respond in this way, God is present and cares for each of us in our times of pain. The stress did not wither her; it seemed to help her blossom for God's glory.

Another friend is "root-bound," or housebound, much of the time as she cares for her brothers with disabilities. When I told her of the opportunity I had to make a sudden surprise visit to one of my sisters, she rejoiced for me. I had been hesitant to tell her, because she had not seen her only sister for over five years. But she was so happy for me! My heart hurt for her and her longing for her sister, and I marveled at the grace and unforced joy with which she delighted in my trip.

This same friend took radiation treatments for skin cancer that had grown too large for surgical removal. Even in that situation and all the unknowns, she said, "I trust in God. Keep praying with me. We have here no abiding city, but we seek one to come."

Leaving her house, I was uplifted by her faith. I had gone to cheer her, but I was the one inspired. She has learned the secret to being bloomed out rather than stressed out. Only, it's not a secret. God clearly shows us how to cling to him and how to view life from an eternal perspective.

The apostle Paul knew what it was to be persecuted, beaten, exhausted, hungry, and in great tribulation. Paul's writing in 2 Corinthians 4 is splendid in his testimony of trust in God despite the trials. So may we also have an inner life that blooms gloriously by God's grace.

prayer

Father, you have never promised that life would be easy, but you have promised to be with me. Because of you I can bloom, whereas on my own I would collapse under stress.

reflection

Do you feel stressed out or bloomed out? How can you manage your schedule to fit in a time of renewal at the feet of Jesus?

2

ARE YOU A HOTHOUSE ROSE?

2 Timothy 2:1-13

Gardens are occasionally battered by severe storms, hail, or wind. We don't plant fragile plants until we're sure they'll survive. Even then we might have to cover them at night. Just as a hothouse plant must gradually learn to face the summer's heat and the cold rains, so I must learn to endure hardness.

It is unrealistic to think that I should never suffer storms. "I just can't take it." "It's impossible to see any good in this situation." "It's not fair." "I don't understand why we have to go through this." These are all things we've thought, heard, or said. No, life isn't fair. But God is good. Great is his faithfulness (Lamentations 3).

Last winter, we didn't move a plant indoors when temperatures dipped below freezing. We were sorry to see that it completely froze and broke off. It had been large and gorgeously full of leaves.

Since watering it regularly this spring, new green shoots are sprouting from the roots, and we're excited to see winter's stress might have strengthened it rather than killed it. Maybe I too can grow stronger and more beautiful when I am stressed and storm-battered. God promises his water will always produce life.

I have heard that while a hothouse rose may be beautiful, it seldom has the fragrance of an outdoor bloom. If I have to be coddled and pampered, I may still be able to experience God's peace and grace, but perhaps I will never be the blessing to others that I should be.

So I should expect to face hardships. The howling winds of grief, the lonely hurt of misunderstanding, or the blackness of depression may assail me. The rocks hurt my feet; the shoes I am called to wear may cause blisters. The journey continues—uphill at that—and I am so tired.

The apostle Paul told Timothy to be strong in Christ's grace. That's my answer too! If I look at the storms, the winding and rough road, the wind and the darkness—I will stumble and fall. To become strong in the pathway of life, I have to learn how to endure hard times. God is faithful to shower me with blessings of joy when I keep my face turned upward toward his sunshine and his rain.

prayer

God, you have not promised a pathway of roses without thorns. But you have promised to be with me every step of the journey. Help me to learn endurance by your grace.

reflection

Does it feel as if life is just too hard? Rather than beg to be sheltered, what steps can you take to become stronger?

3

FLOURISHING AT ANY AGE

Psalm 92

A few years ago my oldest sister, who thrives working with soil, grew her usual large garden in the Midwest. The growing season there is long, so she often plants a fall garden when the spring garden wanes. Usually the heat of the summer takes its toll on the plants and they wither. But if she plants again in July, she can expect a lovely fall crop, and fewer bugs with which to contend.

That particular year the weather was extreme, with high temperatures and alternating harsh storms. The rain pounded the soil; then the sun beat down and hardened the earth into clay. Most of the garden didn't do well. The green beans were past their prime, but she decided to let them be, as she didn't need the space. She pulled out the peas and dug potatoes and replanted a few rows with fresh green bean seeds in hopes that these would bear.

The beans soon sprouted and grew despite the weather. A few weeks later they were blooming, and she anticipated the taste of fresh beans. But the new plants hardly bore any beans. Wearily, she walked over to the old patch, thinking it was time to till everything under. Imagine how excited she was to see the old plants once again green and growing! Not only that, they hung thickly with long, crisp beans. She gleefully filled her apron and returned rejoicing to the kitchen.

She pondered those beans for a while. Did they rebloom and bear perhaps *because of* the trials they endured rather than *in spite of them*? Did those winds and storms strengthen the plants so that they suddenly bore fruit? It reminded her of Psalm 92.

Think of that: bringing forth fruit in old age! Many of us secretly groan at the thought of growing old. We scrutinize our hair for strands of white and eye the lotions that promise to ward off wrinkles. Or, like another sister, we deny the need for glasses and prefer to squint at words at arm's length; and when we can't hear someone, we insist they were quietly mumbling. We certainly reject hearing aids.

We don't want to grow old! But God says our productivity doesn't need to end. It just changes. His Spirit can still be growing vibrantly within us, and because of that life, we can bear fruit. At any age.

prayer

Lord, thank you for your promise that we can bear fruit for you no matter how old we are. Keep our hearts young in their love for you.

reflection

Do you fear being too much of a burden when you are old? How can you keep your spirit young?

4

LED, FED, AND WATERED BY GOD

Deuteronomy 32:1-14

*M*oses had a tough job: leading the children of Israel from Egypt to the land of Canaan. Because of their grumblings, disrespect, and disobedience, many lost their lives during the journey. And after all that, Moses was forbidden to enter the Promised Land because of his anger. He once struck a rock instead of speaking to it as God had told him to do.

Still, God loved Moses dearly, and the Bible tells us God buried him (Deuteronomy 34:6). There was never a prophet like Moses, who knew God face-to-face. Moses was 120 years old, and his eyes were still bright and his vitality strong.

I think the key must have been Deuteronomy 32:12: "The Lord alone did lead him." Verse 10 of the same chapter speaks of God finding His people in the desert, leading and instructing them. Moses knew his spiritual life could only be fed and watered by God.

Moses never wavered in his allegiance. God, and God alone, was whom he trusted, to whom he prayed. Over and over and over.

I remember old people I knew as a child. There was a sweet sister who sat in the "amen corner" (the benches to the side of the pulpit), whose full attention was on the sermon. She often chose songs, especially two that, thirty years later, still remind me of her.

There was a neighbor who wanted the oxtail from a butchering. She said it made excellent soup. She always greeted us cheerily and we chatted awhile. We called her husband Grandpa, and I still like the kind of pink lozenges he always kept in his pocket for children after church services.

One last special memory of Grandma Yoder is the breakfast she fixed for me. She was so tiny and frail, yet she happily brewed coffee and toasted bread, not letting me stir from the chair. I was her guest, and I felt pampered. Her joyful spirit invigorated me.

Grandma Miller always brought gifts for us, usually ones she had made. When she could no longer see well enough to do handwork, she still shared what she had: a book or a tiny pitcher from her treasured collection. She was a gifted storyteller and enjoyed listening to my stories just as much. She loved to sing praises to our Lord, and even on her deathbed sang as long as she was able.

I have aunts and uncles nearing the "old-age hilltop." My father-in-law has Parkinson's disease, which has slowed him physically but has caused him to seek and trust God yet more spiritually. Though his steps falter, his faith does not. In their serenity, I sense a faith that has come from years of trusting God through hardships, and peace that contentedly awaits the call of the Lord. Had they not learned to trust God in the prime of life, when strength marked the day and when they had plenty of energy, they would hardly be able to trust God to lead them through the dark valley of life's ending.

My dad has suffered through physical stress, and also through church stress. Sometimes I might think he would be justified to feel bitter about certain situations, but his testimony remains: "I want to serve the Lord until I die."

God bless our aging people who still flourish "to shew that the Lord is upright" (Psalm 92:15). Truly their lives are a beautiful testimony to the grace of God! Let us grasp that grace so that we too may become strong through difficulties, to bring forth fruit in old age.

prayer

Father, you have blessed me with a heritage of faith. Bless all the elderly, and keep their hearts in your grace.

reflection

What can you do to encourage an elderly friend or relative today?

5

ROOTS DEEP OR SHALLOW?

Colossians 2:1-12

A few years ago our minister planted a small grove of citrus trees. Anxiously, he watered, fertilized, and waited for fruit to form and mature. One day he noticed that a lemon tree was wilting. He watered it heavily for several days, assuming the hot, dry summer had taken its toll on the young tree.

Still the leaves withered. While puzzling over the problem, he shook the tree. Imagine his shock when it fell over in his hand! He lifted the sapling and discovered the underlying cause was not drought or lack of nutrition. Gophers had tunneled beneath the tree and nibbled off the roots completely!

Likewise, if I don't have roots that are deeply grounded in God, I will gradually succumb to spiritual decay. Satan is like those gophers. He will tunnel away at my faith and bring doubts and despair, destroying my peace.

During times of tornadoes in the Midwest, trees were often blown over, or if their roots were firm, the tops were twisted off. I wonder—how does my heart look after a storm?

Beginning each day with prayer and Bible study provides a solid understanding of the Word. The more I read of God's will for us and listen to his Spirit whispering to my heart, the deeper and stronger my roots will grow. "That Christ may dwell in your hearts by faith; that ye, being rooted and grounded in love, May be able . . . to know the love of Christ, which passeth knowledge, that ye might be filled with all the fulness of God" (Ephesians 3:17-19).

Daily trials will come, and winds of stress will shake me. Am I rooted and grounded in love if I become irritated at family members for spilling chili on the new tablecloth or biking across freshly planted rosebushes or forgetting to add the yeast to the bread dough and spoiling the last of the flour?

Life is full of interruptions. Many times I face unavoidable delays: sick children, rainy days, accidents, and misunderstandings. How I face these stresses proves my root strength or reveals my weakness. May I learn to trust God more through each experience.

Most important of all is my morning meeting with my Lord. Without that, things are bound to be tangled. As verse 10 in today's passage says, "[I am] complete in him." Only through Christ's help can my roots be established and my life complete.

prayer

God, by planting my roots deep in your Word, I find growth and stability. Help me to be aware of things that threaten my root system. May I ever be grounded in you.

reflection

Are you quick to doubt the love and grace of God? How can you find stability in him?

6

SOIL MATTERS

Mark 4:1-20

*W*hen we moved to California, we plowed a section of pasture for a garden, but the seeds yielded poorly. It took years of fertilizer and work to build up the soil. Now planting is a joy, because the soil is healthy and produces healthy plants.

How can I have a heart with fertile soil? I need to be open to God. He is the only one who can provide good soil. Surrendering everything—my whole life, soul, mind, and body—is essential to growth. The fertilizer might be a serious study of the Bible and asking faithful Christians to explain verses I don't understand.

A healthy plant is a joy to behold, and a vibrant Christian life is an inspiration to others. I love to be with people who are so clearly rejoicing in the victory and grace of God that their very expression speaks of that relationship. Their closeness to God didn't develop without time and effort.

One of my friends fasts and prays once a week for her family. Not only does that bless her family, but it also nourishes her own soul. My sister has Bible verses posted by her kitchen sink; another always encourages me to look beyond present problems to our eternal God. Another friend writes Bible verses as mottoes and posts them around her house.

I appreciate a church brother's response to "How are you?" He nearly always replies, "The Lord has been good to us." His coworker said of him, "We can always depend on him. When things get hectic he keeps steady." My church brother's soil is healthy, and so is his fruit.

Actively loving the Lord and seeking to learn more about him is the best way to grow. I once read through the four Gospels and kept notes detailing actions and attitudes of Christ. Do I want to be Christlike? It will take a lifetime to learn all that he wants to show me, but I can start today.

A plant will soon show signs of root decay or poor soil. Maybe I would be more conscious of keeping my spiritual life alive and vibrant in Christ if my hair turned purple when my spiritual roots grew unhealthy.

Although I can put up a fake front, like artificial leaves to hide my true self, I can't deceive God. He wants me to be transparent before others also.

Sometimes I need to ask my spouse or my best friend if my "branches" appear healthy and if my "fruit" tastes good. I'm not advocating sweet peaches all day long. Sometimes my fruit needs to be a tangy lemon. Or something salty that makes others thirsty for the water of life. No matter what I am producing, it must be from God and point to him, or it will not be a blessing to anyone, least of all to me.

prayer

Lord, I want my soil to be healthy. Help me to keep it well watered by your Word and nourished by your Spirit.

reflection

What does your life say about the soil of your soul? How can you fertilize it and build it up in order to become healthier?

7

AN ENDURING HARVEST

1 Peter 1:13-25

My neighbor has a beautiful flower garden. It's not cultivated in tidy rows or beds, but rather is strewn among enormous rock formations. The jagged outcroppings of rock jut into the sky, and at the base are glorious colors of the rainbow, with much greenery to soften the stone face.

She digs and plants and scatters—bulbs, plugs, and seeds. We went to see what was growing last week, and I was tempted to go back with a good book and spend the day among the blooms. It's therapeutic to wander along the paths that she says God made, and made to rest in the splendor of leaf and blossom.

During the hot summer the flowers fade, but they'll bloom again when the winter rains come. Hope is the promise that keeps my friend digging, planting, and sowing.

My life is like those flowers. In the whole space of eternity, my years on earth are few and short. But God hasn't promised us only life here on a temporal earth. He has promised us life everlasting, with hope of a wonderful future.

I will be judged by the seeds I plant while I am on earth. If I strive to be pure and holy, I will plant pure and holy seed. That seed will yield a pure and holy harvest. I have never cultivated a love for ornamental pear trees, and maybe it's because I think a pear tree should bear pears, not just be ornamental. So should my spiritual life bring forth fruit for God and not just be a beautiful plant.

The verses in today's reading talk of being born again and of having God's incorruptible seed within. I have a soul that will never die, a life that will live on eternally.

All the earthly things I may plant, even staunch maple trees or hearty oaks, will someday die. But my soul will never die. If I cling to the life that is eternal, the life that is God, I will be with him eternally.

The words in 1 Peter 1:23 and 25 are clear. The word of the Lord will endure forever. It is hard to grasp a picture of forever. I think in terms of time: minutes, hours, days, months, and years. Seasons come and seasons go, just as God promised in Genesis 8:22. But then I notice the beginning of that verse: "While the earth remaineth," it says in the King James Version.

This reminds me of 2 Peter 3, which speaks clearly of a time when this earth will pass away. How then shall I live? I must live in the moment, for it is all I have. But I must live with an eternal perspective, for it is what I place in God's hands that counts at the end.

I can ever grow more like him on my journey here, seeking to brighten my world. The last verse in the epistle of Peter leaves a challenge: "But grow in grace, and in the knowledge of our Lord" (2 Peter 3:18). He lives forever and I can live with him!

prayer

Thank you, God, that you always were, and always will be, even though I cannot understand how it can be so. I trust in you to help me use my mortal time to grow in my soul the things that are immortal.

reflection

Does the brevity of time and mortal life frighten you or encourage you? How can you grow a life that will stand in eternity?

1

GOD IS THE TRUE LIGHT

John 1:1-5

Sunshine—what a glorious gift from God. "Truly the light is sweet, and a pleasant thing it is for the eyes to behold the sun" (Ecclesiastes 11:7). Without light, plants die, and humans nearly do. Some people suffer from seasonal affective disorder, appropriately known as SAD. It's a depression that usually strikes during the short, dark winter days when there is less sunlight. According to one survey, areas with excessive rain and fog have high rates of suicide, which psychologists attribute to the climate.

But in our part of California we have many more days of sunshine than of clouds. Does that mean that we are always cheerful and bright?

We cannot control the sunshine and rain, even though we can usually choose where we live. But more importantly, we can—and must—expose our souls to the light of God. Jesus is the light of the world (John 8:12; 9:5).

I looked in *Strong's Exhaustive Concordance of the Bible* and was nearly blown away by the references to light. I measured the entry for *light*: it is almost twenty-two inches long, with twelve references in one inch. This does not include derivatives of the word—there are many more mentions of *lighten*, *enlighten*, and so on. Do the math. God is serious about this! He wants to be Light for us.

I once faced a major decision: Would I teach in a school I was used to, with younger students I knew and loved? Or would I transfer to a new school, teaching older students, many of whom I did not know? As I agonized and prayed, God lit the path he wanted me to take. Some of the light came from the counsel of older Christians. Some shone into my heart by searching the Bible. I thank God for lifelong friendships that sprang from my choice. Following God's light brought peace and a multitude of blessings.

In our Scripture reading, verse 4 says "In him was life; and the life was the light of men." God's life, sent through his Son Jesus, is our light. I enjoy living in sunshine physically. But more importantly, I long to live in his eternal sunshine spiritually.

What the Bible says about light will astonish and bless you. God's light is life for us. Without him, life truly is too gloomy for words.

prayer

Thank you, God, for sending Jesus to be our light. Help us to keep our faces turned toward this blessed light so that we may live.

reflection

Are you feeling God's sunlight in your heart? Open the blinds and let the rays of his blessed sun warm your soul.

2

OPEN YOUR HEART TO GOD'S LIGHT

John 3:16-21

*G*enesis 1 informs us that the first thing God made was light. God knew that without light a glorious world would still be uninhabitable and unseen.

So he made natural light. During the fall and winter months, when days shorten, at least in the Northern Hemisphere, we see less of that natural light than during the spring and summer. Sometimes it's difficult to feel energized when it's dark outside, and yet the clock declares it's time to get to work.

My sister's friend has struggled with her eyesight for years. She underwent hours of vision therapy, which has changed her life. Still, she finds it hard to see when light is dim. In the evening, as the sun goes down, her range of vision narrows. As long as she has good headlights on the car, she can still drive. But she has backed into a tree, missed a correct road, and narrowly missed driving over children camping in the yard—all because she was lacking light.

Spiritually, God is the light of the world. When I am walking into a scary situation or down an unfamiliar path, God is as near to me as any headlight or any flashlight, and much more dependable.

His is a light that never wanes, never dims. His light shines into the darkness. Imagine a spotlight beaming into a shadowy alley. Suppose the occupants of the alley didn't notice the light. This sounds unreasonable, but the Bible states that God's light is not always noticed, and his light is far brighter than the highest beam of spotlight.

Why doesn't the darkness understand the light? Might it be that alley dwellers are so focused on surviving undercover that they fail to see flashes of light? I also can become so accustomed to my devious sin and fail to recognize God's purifying light.

I long to let his light shine into each corner of my heart—even into the dismal, secretive hideouts. When all that I am and know is revealed in the light of his glory, I will cry out for cleansing. He not only shows where we need to change and how to be clean, but also offers to do the cleaning. What an amazing God!

Just as the woman who took vision therapy had to admit she had a problem, so I must realize that I need God's help. There is no need to be ashamed of God seeing my depravity. He knows everything. If I give it all to him, I am amazed at how bright my world becomes.

God shines to be my light. He wants me to walk in his light, which is simply learning to study, believe, and obey his Word, the Bible.

prayer

Lord, today I ask you to show me if there are any shadowy places in my heart. Shine your holy, blessed light into those corners and bring cleansing. I want to be open to your light.

reflection

Do you fear darkness? Check your vision. Does it need the light therapy of God and his Word?

3

REFLECTION OF GOD'S LIGHT

John 1:1-8

*M*y grandma saved letters from her grandchildren to read again when she grew old. But those hopes faded along with her eyesight when macular degeneration gradually stole her vision. Still, her face was alight with the light that comes from within, a life that reflected Jesus.

My sister's church group sang in a poverty-stricken area of her city one afternoon. A wrinkled and tired face pushed up near the preacher's. "You people," she said, "what is it about you?" She pushed away her matted hair from a cheek that likely hadn't seen soap in a while. "It's almost like you, like you . . ." Three teeth glimmered in a wide grin. "It's like you shine!"

The pastor smiled. "If we shine, it's like the moon that reflects the light of the glory of the sun, only our Son is the Son of God."

"That's it," the woman agreed. "I can feel it and I can see it."

In today's Bible passage we read of a man who was sent by God to witness of the Light. We don't know much about John, only that he faithfully, doggedly, told the crowds to prepare their hearts to meet Jesus, the light of the world. How did he bear witness? He preached and taught about Jesus, the perfect Lamb of God, who was coming to take away the sins of the world.

Some who heard this message were perhaps of the many who longed and prayed for the promised deliverer. The Jews knew and believed the promises from the Old Testament. God would send a Savior, one who would deliver them from Roman rule.

A few of them thought John must surely be the Messiah, the Savior. When he assured them that he was only the forerunner of the Savior, they berated him for preaching and baptizing (John 1:19-28). John was undeterred, even at great risk to himself. He didn't stop declaring the message of the glory that was to come—the glory that was Jesus.

We who have seen God's light and felt it shining into our hearts are called to let others know about that light. This means telling other people what Jesus can do, and about his light that brings life and cleansing to lives clouded by sin.

When I was with my grandma, I almost forgot she was blind because her soul was so brilliant with God's light. And like my sister's singing group, we are not the light, but we can reflect his light.

prayer

Dear Lord, today may I be a faithful light that points the way to you, the true light of the world.

reflection

What is your reflection showing to your family and to your neighbors?

4

GOD'S LIGHT TRANSFORMS

John 1:1-14

While deep-cleaning her son's bedroom, my sister was struck by how dimly lit the room was. One low-wattage bulb swung from the ceiling. She grabbed a flashlight to shine light deeper into the messy closet. Horrors—what was this? A spilled coffee mug with . . . what? Remnants of a meal he had taken to school a long time ago. Many of us with teenagers have found surprises like this. My sister gagged as she scraped out the moldy, maggot-infested pile. As soon as that was done, she replaced the 40-watt bulb with a 75-watt one and hung a light from the closet door. The whole place was transformed.

God's light changes our lives. Completely. If we receive him, the true Light, he gives us power to become God's sons and daughters. To receive him simply means opening our hearts to his light and his salvation. We acknowledge and confess all our sins, asking him to come into our hearts.

We may not be in the lineage of Jesus, but we can be God's children by being born of him. All who come to him in sincerity he will receive. The Bible says he will receive "to them that believe on his name" (John 1:12).

In the years Jesus walked the literal earth, his own people, the Jews, did not receive him. Only a few believed Jesus was the Son of God. Most rejected his message because they had been taught to follow Hebrew laws. They also were looking for an earthly kingdom, but God's kingdom is heavenly. He reigns in hearts, not on thrones.

Jesus came to bring peace. It is a peace that overwhelms our souls because our sins are taken away by Jesus' blood. We are his children, and he keeps us in his light and safety.

The apostle John, who wrote this book of the Bible that bears his name, tells how he beheld the glory of Jesus. It was awesome. It changed his life.

Are we to be pitied because we weren't around to see the flesh-and-blood Jesus? No, we are privileged to know Jesus in our hearts, to hear him speaking to our spirits, and to feel his peace. He still transforms lives.

prayer

Dear Lord, thank you that I can be your child and for your transforming light. Thank you for showing me your glory, in your Word and in your world.

reflection

Is your world transformed by God's light? How can you show his light today?

5

GOD'S STOPLIGHT

Acts 9:1-9

One night, when I was staying in a city, I heard a helicopter flying low. I walked out to the lawn and looked up. I had no idea the pilot could see me, but suddenly a flash of light nearly blinded me and a voice boomed, "Go back into the house!" I stopped in my tracks and immediately obeyed.

In our reading today, Saul was also stopped by a light. He was a persecutor of the Christians and a terror to any who believed on Jesus, to any who walked in God's light. He had no idea how powerful that light was. In Acts 22, Saul, now called Paul, gave his testimony of that enlightening experience on the Damascus Road. He wrote, "I could not see for the glory of that light" (verse 11).

Have I ever been blinded by God's light? Humbly struck to the ground, in awe and devotion, praising and worshiping the light of the world? If not, maybe I have never come out from the shadows.

Coming to the light means letting go of our tendency to hide from God. When I snap on a light or light a lantern, what happens to the previous darkness? It's gone. If I walk outside on a cloudy, moonless night, it's completely dark until I switch on a light. As long as the light shines, there isn't any darkness right where I am. It's my choice.

"We wait for light, but behold obscurity. . . . We grope for the wall like the blind." Isaiah 59 gives a depressing view of life without God's light. It gives the reason for our human despair without God in verses 12 and 13: "Our sins testify against us: . . . In transgressing and lying against the Lord, and departing away from our God. And in verse 16: "There was no man . . . no intercessor." That's our experience without Christ. So empty, so sad, so completely alone.

But that's not the end of the story! Isaiah 60 begins with a triumphant, glorious cry: "Arise, shine; for thy light is come, and the glory of the Lord is risen upon thee. For, behold, the darkness shall cover the earth, and gross darkness the people: but the Lord shall arise upon thee, and his glory shall be seen upon thee. And the Gentiles shall come to thy light."

I am thankful that his light has stopped me, shone around me, and guided me back to the brightness of life.

prayer

Dear God, for all of us, Jews or Gentiles, you have come. Thank you that your light reaches each one of us. Keep us enlightened by your power.

reflection

Has God's light stopped you in your tracks? Share your testimony with someone this week.

6

GOD'S LIGHT— BRIGHTER THAN MY SIN

Ephesians 5:6-16

My sister cares for a woman whose life has been one sad story after the next. She faced rejection and deep despair. But when God's light shone into her heart, she started to see with spiritual vision. Although it isn't easy for her to understand every passage of the Bible, she absorbs it like a sponge and has memorized many verses. The questions she voices after daily study are an amazing testimony to God's light. God has opened her heart to receive his love and forgiveness. Her life, transformed by the blood of Jesus, challenges those who meet her.

Truly, God is a light that can cleanse my gross shamefulness. When I come to him, open and transparent, he reveals the shadows and murky corners I keep hidden in my heart. I might hope God won't find my cherished sin, but he calls, "Fling open the door! Let me shine into that secret place."

But I have to make that first step toward the light of God's grace. "Awake thou that sleepest, and arise from the dead, and Christ shall give thee light" (Ephesians 5:14). Sleeping spiritually means death to my soul. I have to consciously wake up! Arise! Choose life! God's eternal life!

In today's Scripture passage, we read that, yes, we were walking in darkness, but not anymore. I am now in God's light, so I must walk in his light. His life within me helps me to walk acceptably.

He reminds me to keep away from the depraved or misguided deeds of those not following Christ. Don't go to places where people are into evil activities. Keep out of the gloom, and walk in the brightness of the day.

We all have days when we are overwhelmed by the sins of others and things we hear about. Sometimes it seems the darkness is so big it will cover the whole world and extinguish any appearance of light. It can soon seem oppressive to life.

Is God's light so easily dispelled? No. In fact, his light dispels the deepest midnight and utmost debauchery. No matter how dark it is, when God shines in, it's bright.

prayer

Thank you, Lord, that your light is greater than the darkness around us. Help me to cling to your brightness today and to show that light to those I meet.

reflection

Are you troubled by wrong in the world, or in the life of someone you love? Pray for God's light to transform and change.

7

GOD'S LIGHT
OF PEACE

John 9:1-25

On some days, mental fog is like an impenetrable cloud. My sister battled depression with a darkness that threatened to overwhelm her. A huge cloud hovered, waiting to envelop and smother. Even reading a newspaper proved too stressful, too sad. Daily, hourly, she pleaded for God to show her light. Days passed full of hopelessness, and nights were tormented. Still her illness seemed to keep her in the shadows. Finally, a brief ray of light shone through. Confirmations of God's love and care brought her comfort.

The story of the man born blind made a tremendous impression on her. Jesus said the man was born blind so that God's glory could be revealed. Then Jesus healed the man, bringing a life-change of hope and sight. My sister prayed, "Lord, I too will live in the shadows for years if that is what you ask of me. Only may your glory be revealed and your light shine in me."

Her faith grew in the times of depression as it had never flourished in the sunshine. Although she never wishes to repeat the experience, she deeply felt God's care and light that brought her through.

"For with thee is the fountain of life: in thy light shall we see light" (Psalm 36:9). In his light, I too can see light. Even when it's dismal outside, when it rains or snows and days are foggy and dreary, I know the sun is shining behind the clouds. Even when the future is uncertain, when sin is widespread, when I am scared to be alone at night and I lock doors and pull the blinds, *even then* God is the light.

Just as a sunny day makes my workday seem brighter and perks up the drooping poppy, so God's light sweetens my cares and opens blossoms that would otherwise wither under the clouds. It is a wondrous thing for my spiritual eyes to see God's Son.

God's light is unlimited. If he is in my heart, then he is in my home. If he is in my home, then he is in my work. If he goes with me to work, then God is there to shine for me when I feel a shadow falling across my pathway. His light shows me the way to move forward in faith.

When I lack natural light, I start hunting for a lamp switch or a kerosene lantern. Spiritually, may I always look for the light of God's Word to guide me and brighten my path. Light is a blessed thing, and spiritual light is even more blessed. I cannot walk without God's light, or I will stumble and fall. But if I do walk in his light, there is life and there is comfort.

prayer

Dear Lord, I cannot live without your light. I cannot walk unless your light and your glory surrounds me. Shine on my path, and show me your glory. Amen.

reflection

Is there gloom or a shadow in your life and on your path? Seek to know God's light, and ask other Christians to help you find his light when things simply look too painful and grim.

1

DON'T POUT!

Psalm 42

By nature, I tend to withdraw when I feel ignored, offended, or weary. It's easier to sit in a corner and feel sorry for myself than to find joy in my surroundings. When I was much younger I could go for days speaking only a few words, although I was and am usually a chatterer.

When I started teaching school, I soon realized that a teacher cannot be effective while yielding to negative emotions, nor can any daughter of God, no matter what her occupation. Daily I prayed that God would help me to rise above my feelings and find reasons to praise him. With grace, he answered and granted me courage to live, not just by my feelings in the moment, but by the truth. That lesson has helped me in all the years since.

I like to find Bible characters who had the same temperament as I do. That's why I can relate to Elijah. In 1 Kings 18, Elijah went through a literal mountaintop experience. He challenged the priests of Baal, who spent most of the day crying out to the idol, and in the end God showed his marvelous power. The chapter ends with all the people worshiping in awe before the only true God. Victory was swift and dramatic.

But it didn't last long! Soon Elijah was running for his life, and despair gripped his soul. Discouragement dripped from each pore of his being. He sat under the juniper tree and gave in to despondency. But God, in mercy, sent an angel to feed and encourage him.

God is here. God is good. If I stumble around morosely, I am, in effect, showing that God is not enough for me. What an arrogant attitude that is! Faith relies on God for strength, even for the smile that I cannot muster alone.

Sometimes I feel as if I am the only one who cares about a situation; the only one who works for a cause. But if I search, God shows me that others care. Others are working too. In Elijah's case, he thought he was the only one serving God, while God told him that there were seven thousand Israelites who had not bowed to Baal.

I appreciate the psalms of David. No matter how discouraged he was or how tired of running from enemies, he always ends his lines with praise. So then can I, when I feel less than joyful, ask myself, "Why are you cast down, O my soul? Hope in God. He is my rock and I will praise him."

Someone claims that you're a hypocrite if you act joyful when you feel grumpy, but God says, "Choose joy." Hebrews 13:15 tells how: "By [Jesus] therefore let us offer the sacrifice of praise to God continually, that is, the fruit of our lips giving thanks to his name."

It takes a sacrifice of my will to thank him when I feel out of sorts. When I praise him, he will honor and accept that sacrifice and reward me with the emotion of joy. He helps me to speak graciously when I would rather clam up. There's really no reason to pout.

prayer

Dear Lord, I am sorry for the times I give in to the negative emotion of moodiness. Today I choose to praise you for delivering me from myself. I choose to be joyful because you love me.

reflection

Do you ever struggle with moodiness? The next time you are tempted, find reasons and ways to praise God instead.

2

I WOULD NEVER ENVY, WOULD I?

Psalm 73

I have watched others turn all their labors into profitable enterprises; they are the kind of people that turn everything they touch into money. Aren't we serving the Lord too? Why then do we have to scrape and pinch to meet the monthly payments? It doesn't seem fair.

King David found himself battling the enemy within—envy toward the wicked, because it seemed as though all went well for them. They prospered in strength and wealth while he struggled for his life. It wasn't fair! He served and honored God while they blasphemed him.

David admitted that he was thinking wrongly. When he sought God's presence, and listened to him, he realized that the end of the wicked is destruction. Why would he envy someone who was heading the wrong direction? In God alone, he concluded, is strength and trustworthiness.

Keeping my eyes on God is essential to maintaining a proper attitude about others. Most of the people I am tempted to envy are other Christians. Maybe they're voted in for a job I think I'm good at, while I have no responsibilities other than showing up for church services and other activities. In fact, that exact scenario happened a few years ago. I found myself thinking the ideas of those in charge were strange and inefficient. I was stunned when God showed me I was jealous.

Thank God for his forgiveness and peace. When I repented of the feelings of envy, I could fully and cheerfully support everything the committee members suggested. I didn't need to add any of my own ideas but rather entered wholeheartedly into their plans. It was a blessing to work with them. In my change of heart, I acknowledged my sin and began to pray for the leaders and for all the decisions they faced.

Years ago I found myself envious of families who had a variety of girls and boys. At that time we had one daughter and three sons, which was beautiful, but how I longed for another daughter. One day I was complaining inwardly about the names of the newborn baby girls. Suddenly I stopped and asked myself, why do I care? The naked truth was that I envied them their little girls. How foolish! God gives us our families, as he desires, for his glory and for our edification. I surrendered my desire and found peace. Truly, if I follow the path of the Spirit, I will have love toward all. "Let us not be desirous of vain glory, provoking one another, envying one another" (Galatians 5:26).

One antidote for envy is contentment. My sister is a challenge to me in this. She has a small house that must seem crowded with five children bouncing about, but she is joyful and serene. Recently a close friend visited her and was astonished: "I had no idea you lived in such a tiny place." That my sister had never talked about the lack of a roomy house spoke loudly to me of her contentment and total lack of envy.

prayer

Lord, I am sorry for times when I envy another's accomplishments or progress. I want to share your values and see your truths. Before you, I am loved and accepted. I choose to "rejoice with them that do rejoice and weep with them that weep."

reflection

If you are feeling disgruntled toward someone, consider: Are you jealous in some way? Counter that feeling with genuine warmth from God's love.

3

THE UGLINESS
OF PRIDE

James 4

Sometimes I am tempted to think, why shouldn't I be proud? I have accomplished so much today. Shouldn't I feel good about that? Perhaps a healthy self-esteem, and gratitude to God for granting me health and a sound mind, is different from pride.

God has a clear way to bring me back to reality. I like to think I'm organized. Well, really? Our Monday night's sleep was shattered when the phone rang. "Weren't you going to meet us at the airport?" Chagrined, we admitted we hadn't turned the day-timer calendar for the week and had completely forgotten about our friends' flight that night. They live in Central America and had come to the States for a long visit. How could we have missed that important day? Bless their hearts, they patiently waited for us for an hour and are still our friends.

Pride can ruin relationships. If I insist that my ideas are better and must be followed, I break the peace. If I run heedlessly over another's plans, it shows that I think more highly of my plans and do not love as Christ loves.

"Only by pride cometh contention: but with the well advised is wisdom" (Proverbs 13:10). Perhaps today we'd say, "Wisdom is found in those who take advice." It is a little startling to realize that most of my problems in relationships come from pride. If I am humble enough to accept counsel, I can gain wisdom and the end result is peace.

The chapter in James is clear. Humility is a deliberate act. Pride sometimes sneaks unwittingly upon me, but to be humble is a conscious act.

The first step to humility involves my heart's response to our great and awesome God. When I bow before him and catch a glimpse of his holiness and power, and I see myself as I am, a poor mortal, lost without him, what response can there be but humility?

Humility is elusive. If I think have attained it, I have in reality lost it. Spending time alone to worship and revere God is the way to find victory over pride. When I enter the workaday world, I must carry with me the picture of my own unworthiness.

God hates pride. Proverbs 6:16-17 says that even a proud look is an abomination to him. If I look disdainfully at another's clothes, car, house, or even a dish they bring to the potluck, it shows a proud heart. How I dress myself or my child—whether it is a color or hairstyle that screams "Look at me!" or is in a humble manner that draws people's minds to God—reveals what's in my heart.

Pride pushes up its ghastly head in small, seemingly harmless ways. Once at our church's carry-in meal, a friend underestimated the time it would take for potatoes to soften in a large casserole. I thought to myself, "Don't you know that you have to increase the cooking time when you multiply a recipe? You just start the cooking sooner—how simple!"

It was only six months later when I was the one who delayed the fellowship meal. The rice just wouldn't soften. I ate lots that day, but not rice. The words I hadn't said, but thought, came back to mock me. Over and over I was humbled. Just rice? No, God's lesson in humility.

How I interact with others also shows if I am proud or humble. May I be courteous, smiling, and kind, showing that God's love and humility fill my heart. Deferring to others shows that I love my neighbor as myself, a command of God that demonstrates true humility.

prayer

Lord, you alone are worthy of honor. Help me to be humble before you, and to let that humility guide my actions and words.

reflection

Do you feel your way is better? Show humility by deferring to someone else's plan this week.

4

IT'S ALL ABOUT ME

2 Corinthians 8

My family has been blessed by unselfishness acts of others. When we're traveling, our lawn gets mowed, the chickens are fed, and the mail is gathered. Often someone brings a dish of food for our first night at home. When we had to leave suddenly for an emergency, someone took care of all the loose ends I was frantically trying to tie before we left. Just yesterday a very busy man helped me with a technological difficulty in the middle of his day. That was a true act of unselfishness.

I was surprised to find that the Bible doesn't use the word *selfishness* at all. Yet it alludes to it many times. Selfishness is thinking of my own needs and comforts, my own ideas and plans. It wants me to prosper regardless of how I might hurt another on my way to success.

Proverbs 6 lists various ways I can be selfish. If I do not pay what I owe, if I give less than I promise, if I harm another's reputation, if I spread unkind or untrue rumors, if I withhold good when I have opportunity to share, if I bring trouble to my family—all these show a selfish heart.

Giving money isn't so hard when I have plenty. But what about when finances are tight? The Corinthians were sharing what little they had to help others. There will always be someone who has less than I do. If I wait until I have much, I will probably never learn to give.

Giving of my time can be the most unselfish act of all. Sometimes it would be easier to throw a twenty-dollar bill at someone than to stop to listen to his story. I have precious memories of spending

Mondays with another family. It was the husband's day off, so my husband arranged his schedule to fit. Was it a day wasted? Perhaps, if we count accomplishments. But in a relationship it was invaluable. One cannot put a price on friendship.

I have discovered that if I don't rush through a grocery store, but rather take the time to look people in the eye, to smile and say hello, many times I will have occasion to share God's love. If I open my heart and my schedule, God will bring opportunities and the grace to bless others for his glory.

At home I have many opportunities to show unselfishness. Once my family planned a fishing trip but I thought I had too much to do. Thankfully, I realized work always waits and I joined my family. That evening is now a special memory, whereas I certainly can't recall the job I so desperately thought I should do.

I think of my mother's example of fixing food the way Dad liked it. She always made apple dumplings without syrup—just half of an apple dabbed with butter and cinnamon and wrapped in flaky dough. With my father's diabetes, she skipped the sugar, which each could add as desired. When I was married and paging through new cookbooks, I spied a recipe with syrup cooked and poured over the dumplings before baking. They were delicious. Excited, I told my mom. Smiling, she said, "That's how I grew up eating them, but your dad preferred them without the syrup, even before he had diabetes."

I was humbled. That's being unselfish. Life truly isn't about me.

prayer

Heavenly Father, you have done so much for me. Open my eyes to see opportunities to help others with the love you share with me. Keep me from selfishly guarding my possessions and my time. They are yours. Use them for your glory to bless others.

reflection

How can you open your schedule today to reach out kindly to show unselfish love to someone?

5

JUST HURRY UP!

2 Peter 1:1-11

By nature, I am not patient. My father sometimes dubbed me "Do It Now." Why should I wait? If we know what is to be done, if we agree on how to do it, well, then let's just do it.

But in life I daily work with people. It's not fair to a family to rush, rush, rush through life. I learned years ago that it isn't in anyone's best interest to hurry children. It is better to awaken them earlier and take a longer, leisurely route than to have everyone frustrated by my impatience.

The work of patience cannot be completed overnight. It takes patience to learn patience. In Luke 21:19, Jesus says, "In your patience possess ye your souls." From that I understand that patience begins in my spirit. And when patience rules my spirit, it is evidenced by my response to life and all its interruptions.

Hebrews 10:36 reads, "Ye have need of patience," and I often sense that need within my soul. Once I was frustrated because the children weren't hustling the way I thought they should. They leisurely ate breakfast and got dressed, and tided the house very slowly. We had a few baskets of laundry waiting to be hung on the line, so I grabbed one and headed outside, muttering a few choice words that I hoped would hurry the children a bit. I knew I was feeling disgruntled and thought I should step outside lest I say something I would regret.

Suddenly I found myself singing a children's song, one they had been singing a lot. "This little light of mine, I'm gonna let it shine." As I sang, the Holy Spirit convicted me. Where was my light? It certainly was not shining. Tears streamed down my face as I ran indoors to find the children and tell them I was sorry for my impatience. They sweetly forgave me, and smiling, bounced out the door to go to school. "Let it shine, let it shine, all the time."

Sometimes I get impatient with God. After praying for a situation for years, it is hard to keep waiting on his answer. But the Word is clear: "Wait on the Lord: be of good courage, and he shall strengthen thine heart: wait, I say, on the Lord" (Psalm 27:14).

Patience may never come naturally, but by the supernatural power of God, I can learn to wait on him and to show patience to my family, friends, and all people.

prayer

Dear Lord, you have been so patient with me. Thank you, and help me today to show patience with everyone I meet, especially the people with whom I live. Teach me to wait on you with grace and courage.

reflection

What can you do to stay calm and wait when you're faced with a waiting time?

6

BUT I'M SO SCARED!

Psalm 91

*W*hen we first moved to California, we asked the neighbors about the danger of rattlesnakes. Yes, the snakes are here; yes, they are dangerous. Unlike the bite of a Missourian copperhead, which we were used to and didn't always require antivenom, a rattlesnake's bite must be treated, and treated fast.

The fifty-two-acre property we purchased was overgrown with weeds, blackberry bushes, and poison oak. Any number of snakes could be hiding in the bushes and tall grass.

Another potential danger was the pond. The children knew they were not permitted to go to the pond alone. But they rambled all over the woods, exploring each rock and stream.

One day I asked my husband if it was wise to let them tramp off by themselves. What if they were bitten by a rattlesnake and couldn't make it back to the house? What if they decided to catch frogs and fell into the pond? What if a mountain lion was lurking, just waiting on a little boy for its dinner?

Wisely, my husband replied, "If you start down the road of fear, there's no stopping point. You may as well stay at home with the doors closed, huddle in a corner, and shiver. The world is full of dangers. But God is everywhere. He will keep the children safe."

Such a profound truth! It brought peace, and I repeat the words when I am tempted to become fearful. It does not mean being careless, but being careful and trusting.

Fear brings confusion, which is not of God, for he is peace. First John 4:18 tells me that perfect love casts out fear. Fear brings torment. But God's love is perfect, and if I love him with all my heart, he will take away my fear.

Many promises in the Bible speak of God's presence, of his care and protection. I must choose whether to believe it. Faith or fear? It's up to me.

When accidents happen, and someone gets hurt or killed, does that mean that God is not doing his job and keeping his promise? We live in a fallen world. Sin has brought pain, illness, and death. Don't blame the Lord. He is *life*. His protection may be spiritual. Even in the midst of danger, God can keep my heart quiet and my trust complete.

prayer

Dear Lord, thank you for being omnipresent, for your promises to be with me no matter what. Teach me to rest in your care. Today, I trust you.

reflection

What are you afraid of? Is it a legitimate fear? Talk to God, and talk to someone you trust.

7

WHAT WILL PEOPLE THINK?

Psalm 27

Surely I don't care what someone might say about me, do I? I'm my own person, following my own ideas, right? But sometimes the fear of what others think creeps upon me in unsuspecting ways. Proverbs 29:25 says: "The fear of man bringeth a snare." That's profound. I wonder what snares it could bring to me?

The snare of flattery. I don't want someone to think poorly of me if I criticize her, so when I am asked for an opinion, I try to speak only in agreement. If I disagree, she might feel angry. I don't want to risk that, so instead I flatter so she will think highly of me. That is, in effect, dishonest. So "the fear of man" from Proverbs can lead to fudging on the truth, turning my response into a lie.

The snare of shame. I am afraid my friend will wonder why I can't host the visitors for a meal, so I push, cajole, and wheedle my family into helping me put on a fancy spread during a very full week. I should be humble enough to admit that it's too much, we can't do it, no matter what it makes others think of me.

The snare of putting on a good front. Is it wrong to want to look good? God does ask me to be orderly, neat, and clean. But if I dress with the foremost motive being to make a good impression, it might be a dishonor to God. Can I clothe myself instead in a way that shows I love God first and most?

The snare of refusing to take a responsibility because I might mess up. God doesn't require perfection, only "a willing mind" (2 Corinthians 8:11-12). In these verses, I am touched by the gentleness of God's words through Paul. I am not accountable to do more than I can, but I am responsible to act on the abilities God has given. He always blesses willingness and availability.

The fear of being hurt. Once I found myself holding back in sharing feelings for fear of being rebuffed. It hurts to open up my heart and then be rebuffed. But friendship is not real if I have to bluff my way through, saying only "I'm fine" and talking only about surface subjects.

I love the last part of Proverbs 29:25: "But whoso putteth his trust in the Lord shall be safe." I tremble, shrink, and cringe when I try to measure up to the standard created by humans. I will never be skinny, beautiful, elegant, or talented enough. But when I totally and completely trust the Lord, I am safe. Safe from dishonest responses, shame, shirking my duties, and being disconnected from reality. God keeps my heart in his will, and his approval is, after all, what really matters.

prayer

Dear God, forgive me when I sin because the fear of others controls me. Teach me to fear you alone, for that is the beginning of wisdom. Keep me strong to do your will, for I am willing to obey you.

reflection

Are you tempted to be shallow in your relationships because of fear? How can you be filled with God's Spirit so that you can be honest and open?

1

IS GOD FAR AWAY?

Acts 17:22-31

When my husband and I were courting, we never ran out of things to talk about. We grew up as neighbors, but we still had a lot to learn about each other. Talking and listening are still important, even after twenty-some years of marriage. It's an excellent way to become close to someone and to stay close.

I think of other relationships—and realize that the time I spend nurturing them is a direct correlation to how close I am to that person.

Being close to God is the most important relationship of all. I have often heard a minister preach that, if our vertical relationship to God is intact and current, then our horizontal relationships—those with other humans—will also be stable.

My uncle Enos often quoted the searching question, "If God seems far away, who moved?" God never changes, so if God feels distant, it must be that I have moved away from him.

I cannot live without God. He has provided a way for us to have close fellowship with him. "But God commendeth his love toward us, in that, while we were yet sinners, Christ died for us. . . . We were reconciled to God by the death of his Son . . . we shall be saved by his life" (Romans 5:8, 10).

The only way to stay close to God is to spend time with him daily, talking to him in prayer and listening to him. I learn what he wants of me by daily study of his words to me: the Bible.

He also speaks to me through his Spirit. "When he, the Spirit of truth, is come, he will guide you into all truth" (John 16:13). The Spirit shows me God's will.

The world is noisy, with many things clamoring for my attention. Even when I am home alone, a timer beeps, a phone rings, an airplane flies overhead, an appliance hums. It can be difficult to find a place where it's truly quiet. But it's essential to my relationship with God.

I often ask God to help me block out the noise. I must learn to be quiet within my soul, and to listen to his Spirit whispering to mine. He helps me to shut out the pressures and the work that's waiting.

This time alone with him actually strengthens me to face those pressures and work. I marvel at the many times during the day that God brings to mind a verse I studied that morning. He pays attention to my needs; can I not pay attention to the Lord?

If I feel distant toward God, I ask myself: Have I failed him in some way? Sin always breaks that closeness, and repentance repairs it. When I spend time with God, he blesses my heart with joy and peace. It's worth every effort.

prayer

Dear Lord, thank you that I can have a close relationship with you. Help me to keep my line of communication open to hear, to listen, and to speak with you.

reflection

How can you take a more active, assertive approach in your relationship with God? Is God your best friend?

2

PARENTS: HONOR THEM

Ephesians 6:1-3

*M*y parents love God and taught me to serve him in words and work. Circumstances were opportunities to learn God's lessons. My parents taught us to glorify God in how we worked and what we wore, read, and spoke. I love my parents and have based many choices on what they would endorse. While I wasn't always respectful, I tried to avoid purposely disappointing them. Even today, when I sew a dress, I think of how my mother taught me to keep it modest and simple. I can respect her teachings even as an adult in my own home.

"Honour thy father and thy mother" is a commandment first recorded in Exodus 20 and often repeated in the New Testament. We read no qualifiers. It's not "Honor them if they are Christian parents," "Honor them if they teach you life skills," "Honor them if they are faithful, kind, committed, and prosperous." No. It simply says, "Honor them."

Even when they are not worthy of honor? Who am I to say if they are worthy or not? God requires me to honor those who gave me life.

Honor is a state of mind and spirit. It means showing respectful deference to my parents. For those whose parents are not following God, honor doesn't mean a blind obedience, especially if parents require something against God's Word. Still, honor extends grace.

Daniel was captured as a young man and taken to Babylon. He respected his parents by obeying the Hebrew law, even at the risk of being killed. Foremost, he honored the God his parents worshiped (see Daniel 1).

Joseph also was committed to serving God, although he too was taken from his father and thrown in among Egyptians. (We read his story in Genesis 37–50.) He was very close to his father, who wept for days when he thought Joseph had been killed. Their joy at being reunited many years later is a picture of true honor and delight.

What if my parents truly hurt me? Some family situations are too horrific for words. But God can still redeem my heart, so in time I can offer forgiveness, and therefore receive grace. Healing may be a painful, lifelong process, but God always honors my choice to obey his directives.

Ephesians 6 reminds us that to honor our parents is the first commandment that came with a promise: "That it may be well with thee and that thou mayest live long on the earth."

Honoring one's parents doesn't guarantee living to a ripe old age, but it does follow that the years I do have will be happier and more blessed. We can all think of situations in which children were injured by acts of disobedience to their parents. Perhaps that is what God's promise means. Or it could simply mean that we will live eternally, for if we obey this commandment, we are honoring God. A life that honors God is rewarded by a home in heaven.

prayer

Lord, thank you for my parents. Thank you for the heritage of faith. May I honor, respect, and obey my parents. I pray for those who do not have a happy childhood to remember. Cover them with your grace, and restore them by your mercy.

reflection

How can you today show that you honor your parents? Call them, write them a letter, and tell your children or other young people stories about them.

3

MY HUSBAND—IS HE MY ALL IN ALL?

Ephesians 5:19-33

I am blessed with an excellent memory. My husband, not so much. Sometimes I think he should know where my favorite bookstore is, but he doesn't. I can remember the first time he bought me a jacket at a yard sale. He says, "What yard sale?" A day is incomplete for me if I don't write. Writing more than a signature on a contract is a misery to him. Can we still be one in Christ?

God likens marriage to Christ and the church. Sometimes I read Ephesians 5 and think, yes, if my husband only treated me as Christ does the church, how blissful my life would be!

But God does not require a human husband to be Christ. He can't be—no more than *I* can perfectly emulate Christ. A husband is, after all, human, living in an earthly family and with an earthly wife.

Expecting from my husband what only Christ can give is a recipe for failure. Only God can always be patient, kind, forgiving, and loving. Only God can always understand. Only God always has time.

When I accept the fact that my husband cannot be all in all to me, it follows that I must learn to find my fullness in Christ. In this way I can still be gracious and loving even when I feel misunderstood. God helps me to act lovingly even when I don't feel like it. Commitment is more important than feelings.

The doctrine of godly submission is often ignored. Who wants to give in, again and again? But the apostle Paul said wives must reverence their husbands, and honor and submit to them. Husbands are accountable to God for the choices they make. I believe wives are accountable to submit. Yes, Colossians 3:18 leaves a clause: "as it is fit in the Lord." Submission does not mean following a husband into sin. May God grant each wife who has an unsaved husband the ability to still honor him and to find wisdom to show grace.

My husband and I have concluded that one key to staying close is never giving the other cause to doubt that he or she is the most important person in your life (after God). My husband comes before my hobbies, my parents, and even before our children.

Sometimes this meant leaving the children with a babysitter while I went to the hardware store with my husband. Or it could mean buying our sons the style of jacket that my husband prefers even when they want another kind.

My husband tries to obey the command in Ephesians 5:25 to love his wife as Christ loved the church. He thinks of me through the day and prays for me, and he knows I am doing the same for him. He asks what I prefer when he's planning our next trip or a major purchase. He calls me when he will be late, and I try to have supper ready when it's most convenient for his schedule. He puts job estimates on hold to hang a shelf for me.

It's not always the big things that try my love and submission. I would willingly give my life for him. But it's the little things that are sometimes difficult. Can I defer to his wishes on which brand of ketchup to buy? Can I cook his favorite dishes even when I dislike them? Can I value his work, his personality, and his earnings by showing honor and respect?

If I do, our marriage will be blessed.

prayer

Heavenly Father, the one who united my husband and me, teach me what it is to be one with you and one with my spouse. Give me grace to submit lovingly and patiently, and make me easy to live with.

reflection

If married, how do you respond when your husband asks you to give up your idea, be it the color of a couch or the make of a vehicle? Ask God to show you a special act of love you can do for your spouse.

4

MY CHILDREN— OR GOD'S?

Colossians 3

I love children, but sometimes I wonder, did I really bargain for all this? Messy rooms, stinky socks, interrupted nights, pine-cone collections, and smudged windows?

But God reminds me, children are a gift! A gift—straight from heaven—that I did not deserve. I look at them and marvel. They are God's, yet he lets me have them in my life. God gives me the awesome responsibility to lead them back to him.

When my children were babies, I had to give them hours of time, love, and care. Otherwise, they would have died. It's that simple! I remember feeling the awe of knowing that this little life was in my hands. I was responsible for it. And I was accountable to God for how I treated this child.

More than feeding and clothing a child, I am responsible to nurture and train. This includes teaching them to love God, honor his Word, and get along with others. My husband and I are blessed with godly parents, and we can freely ask their advice when we face a troubling situation in parenting.

Relationships with young children are relatively easy to establish and maintain. They are naturally trusting, and they think you are the most wonderful person in the world. It's a time of wonder and learning together.

After they grow old enough to dress themselves, I have caught myself neglecting one-on-one time with them. Especially in a large family it can be a challenge to really know each child as an individual.

It takes time to keep up with everyone, but what is more important than the souls of my children? If I make time for them and show them that I truly care about who they are and what they do, it will reap benefits far greater than the time invested.

I enjoy each stage of family life. At one time we had four teenagers. Contrary to what we heard about the tough times had by many parents of teens, we found it a delight. We thank God for the openness we share with our children. It's not a constant battle of wills but a time of discovery and joy because of the redeeming work of God in our family.

When our children were younger, there were days I didn't know if any of us would survive the growing-up years. But God is faithful. If I honestly follow his pattern for child-rearing and do my best each day, acknowledging my failures and my dependence on him, God blesses in ways I never imagined. Studying the book of Proverbs has inspired me with practical directives in child-rearing.

Long ago I heard a prayer asking God to overrule and override in the areas where we fail, and I have prayed that many times. Letting God rule doesn't mean carelessly sailing through this parenting journey, expecting God to fix everything I mess up, but rather it means realizing my accountability to God for how I act toward my children and taking that responsibility seriously.

prayer

Heavenly Father, creator of life, thank you for the children that you have graciously given to me. Help me to lean heavily on you to bring them up in your ways. Keep me alert to their needs, and give me wisdom in each situation to respond with your love and your will.

reflection

How can you show your children or other young people that they belong to God?

5

COOPERATING WITH COWORKERS

Romans 12

*I*t was a miserable day to be out. My friend and I slipped and slid on the icy roads to the turkey farm where we worked. I had hoped to sew a dress that day, in a cozy house, with an abundance of coffee. But here I was. Stuck in a cold, smelly job. Suddenly my friend started singing. I listened to her brave voice and I was convicted of my own negative attitude. I had not been a pleasant companion that day, but she was gracious and forgiving. Soon I was singing with her. That day stands out as one of my favorites on the job.

For those who work daily with others, it can be a challenge to face each day with a gracious spirit. Personalities differ and are fascinating, but are not always agreeing.

Romans 12 describes how God gives each person talents unique to that individual. We need each other. By God's grace, I can learn to build on another's strengths rather than let the differences divide and destroy.

Appreciate what is unique. Does one employee love to chat about small details? That person is possibly gifted to work with precision in areas where another may lose patience.

Is one person quiet and I second-guess her thoughts? Perhaps she shrinks from the limelight and enjoys listening. It is good to learn to ask her opinion. I have been surprised at a quiet person's depth of thought.

Another may plow tirelessly through work. She may be the one who needs to be reminded to take a break. She appreciates being thanked for her labor, even if working hard comes naturally.

If you have time to study the twelve disciples Jesus chose to walk with him on this earth, you will see twelve varying characters, but not one was less valued by our Lord.

I am learning to celebrate the people who fill in at places where I am less skilled. Each of us has limitations. God has arranged for us to work together in love.

At our church sewing circle, two ladies form the committee to keep things organized and gather supplies. I tend to run ahead, and recently I apologized to the other sister on the committee for doing so. A bit astonished, she replied sweetly, "I was just thinking how thankful I am that you go ahead with things. It makes me nervous to be in charge." We both were awed how God arranged for us to work together. Isn't that a beautiful picture of teamwork?

On those days when I feel unappreciated and taken for granted, I pray to be reminded that after all, I am a servant. Even Christ came to minister, and not to be ministered unto (Matthew 20:28).

When I, from my heart, practice Romans 12 and Ephesians 6, I am amazed at how well things go. On the days when I am hurt, or disagree vehemently? Those are the days to extend forgiveness and grace. I long to bless others and, by God's grace, to work with them peacefully.

prayer

Lord, you have given me people to work with. People with souls, personalities, ideas, and attitudes. Help me to nurture relationships with your grace.

reflection

When a coworker disregards your wishes, what will you do to show grace? When that person makes a mistake, will you help to clean the mess, or will you say, "I told you so"?

6

THE CHURCH—
CHRIST'S BODY

1 Corinthians 12

One year the school board couldn't find a teacher for our church-operated school. Finally, when September came, they decided the families would try homeschooling. I taught school before my marriage and loved it. But it was different now. I had six children; the oldest was fourteen and the youngest not yet one. It was hard to teach the lessons besides doing all the housework. I have a great admiration for women who homeschool; may God bless them.

A sister in the church offered to teach for me one morning a week. How did she know I was feeling overwhelmed? Those few hours meant more to me than she will ever know. She was truly caring for me, as God wants us to care for each other in the church.

Through faith in Christ we are adopted into his family. That makes us brothers and sisters. Among my friends, the dearest to me are the ones God placed in the local congregation where I am a member. These are the people I call when I need prayer or beds for unexpected visitors. They are the ones who keep me grounded when I get carried away with an idea. And yes, they are the ones who lighten the burdens that get too large for me.

God calls us to join his church (which he calls his body) and to find a place where we belong. We are all members together, with one goal: to serve him and encourage each other on the journey to heaven.

Christ is the head of the church. He is the brain, if you will. Each member of the body is guided by the brain, down to the smallest toe or blood vessel, doing God's will together. If I can remember that we are one in him with the same goal in view, it helps me to avoid judging another.

God has blessed us with individual gifts. Let us develop them and grow in his grace. Not all can teach well, or sing well, or host company easily. What a blessing it is when we can all work together in a peaceful way, each one doing the part we are chosen to do.

Following the directives in Romans 12 creates an atmosphere of mutual fellowship. "Kindly affectioned . . . with brotherly love; in honour preferring one another." It is easy to defend my blood brother, even when I don't agree with all he does. Can I extend the same defense for my brother and my sister in the church?

Spending time together outside of Sunday services is a good way to develop close relationships with church members. I enjoy working on projects together, or just dropping by for a quick cup of tea. Being part of a group that truly cares about each other is a comfort. If I ask my sisters in the church for advice, they will respond graciously.

I long to build up my sisters, to encourage and inspire them as they do me. Speaking words of confirmation and appreciation strengthens any relationship. God's gift of the church is a mystery (Ephesians 3). I am unworthy to be a part of his mystery, and I thank him for its blessing on my life.

prayer

Dear Lord, you had an image in mind of a perfect bride, a church where all members serve you and bless each other. Help me to faithfully be a part of your bride and to build up relationships and never to destroy.

reflection

This week, find ways to tell five or more sisters in your church what you appreciate about them.

7

DO NEIGHBORS HAVE YOUR BACK?

Romans 13:8-10

Who called?" I asked my husband, as he grabbed his shoes. "Neighbor to the south. Her gate won't open. I'll be right back." He was only home for ten minutes when another neighbor called, worried about water in the backyard.

I could have been frustrated, as our suppertime kept being interrupted. But neighborly relationships come before mealtime. South Neighbor watches out for us too. Once she called while we were on a trip to let us know she had seen a strange truck driving on our property. From the beginning of our friendship she has attended our children's school programs, standing in for their grandparents, who can't travel the distance. She has our back.

It is common for North Neighbor to have a meal waiting for us when we arrive home from a trip. We call each other often and stop in at each other's house for coffee and a pick-me-up. When I feel sad, I can call her. She will understand and care. Since her husband passed away, she joins us for Saturday night pizza and has accompanied us on trips. She's no longer "just a neighbor"; she has become like family.

God has blessed us with these friends who truly look out for us. They aren't part of our church community, but they are very special to us.

It means so much to know that our neighbors will watch out for anything that might hurt or come between us. One day I must have seemed curt to one of my neighbors, and I appreciate that she asked me if she had done something to annoy me. It was my turn to apologize. I had simply been in a dreadful rush and failed to respond graciously. I admire her so much for asking me about it.

As I write this, I realize that the rules for neighbors are the same for any relationship. It involves simply honoring them and showing kindness without expecting anything in return. "Given to hospitality" might mean giving up an hour of my already full day to listen to my neighbor. It may mean stopping on my way to a meeting to give her a ride to town. Sometimes it means my husband postpones my "honey do" list while he repairs an elderly couple's leaky faucet. Do I resent that? No, because I am thankful for the neighbors that God has given, and we want to bless them with the love he has shown to us.

Being a true neighbor is not a constant honey-sweet relationship with those who love us. It is also extending forgiveness to those who don't keep good fences or who race down our lane, throwing gravel in the ditches. It is doing good to any who might do evil to us. "As much as lieth in you, live peaceably with all," Romans 12:18 commands.

prayer

Dear God, thank you for the neighbors you have chosen for me. Help me to extend grace and a helping hand to them whenever I have opportunity. May I show your love as a testimony to those around me.

reflection

This week, what can you do to be a good neighbor? Do you have your neighbors' backs?

1

LOVE THAT CHANGES A LIFE

Galatians 5:14-26; 1 Corinthians 13

Yesterday a neighbor was at my friend's house. Again. This neighbor is an eccentric elderly woman with many health issues and a mental disorder. She is fiercely independent but also loves people. My friend checks on the neighbor regularly since the woman's only son lives far away and has little contact with his mother. She has hardly anyone to care for her, so she has adopted herself into my friend's family.

Although my friend has a full schedule, her heart of compassion opens the door to her house and to her heart. In fact, she testifies she has learned lessons of acceptance from the neighbor. That's true love—love that shows grace, day after weary day.

My sister also shows God's love to the many who come needing a boarding place. Her doors are always open, and so is her heart. One boarder in particular is not easy to care for. My sister takes her to doctor visits, keeps track of her medication, and listens to her stories that tell of a life filled with pain and horror. I see Jesus' love mirrored in my friend and in my sister.

The fruit of God's Spirit begins with love. Selfless agape love encompasses all the other attributes. Agape love is divine, originating only from God and from his life within me. While it isn't sensual, emotional, or temperamental, it does affect my emotions, and my temperament will certainly be tempered by this love.

First Corinthians 13 gives us a glorious, challenging picture of love—God's love. A disciple of Jesus passionately loves God, and in turn God's love in my heart will change my life.

Love is not looking out for myself, but rather looking out for the good of others. In a simple word, love is kind. Kindness shows benevolence and goodwill toward others. It is thoughtful and sensitive.

Love doesn't envy what another has, does, or is. Love is contented with God's provisions and the way he made me. Finding my fulfillment in God is the key to this contentment.

Love is not proud or boastful about what I have or can do. Love defers to other people's desires and ideas when it's possible. I like my own ideas, and I want others to like them too. But true love seeks to honor others by listening to their suggestions and following them. I was excited about a great menu idea for our church picnic. But my friend on the committee had an even better idea, and it brought my heart peace to tell her so.

Love doesn't find even the smallest bit of glee in hearing that someone else is in trouble, even when it's the person I most struggle to like. Love longs to see everyone walking in victory. It is also a test of my love when I can truly rejoice in another's success.

Love bears the daily balance of life, believes in God fervently, shares a hope for eternal joy, and endures faithfully every day.

prayer

Dear Lord and Master, today may my life be saturated with your love, so that it might flow to others freely, abundantly, and beautifully.

reflection

What can you do today to show unselfish love to someone who is unable to reciprocate?

2

NOT JUST HAPPY, BUT JOYFUL

Isaiah 61

A dear friend of mine is a true example of joy. Years ago, a group of youth had an impromptu supper at her house. It didn't matter what we ate, because the atmosphere was so welcoming and happy. She came to check on the food supply, and her rippling laughter soon had the rest of us joining in. "Praise the Lord that the crackers are gone," she said, her face crinkling with true joy. Everyone had a cracker for their soup, and it was "just enough."

She is still smiling. For years, she cared for her husband, whose once-brilliant mind was failing with dementia. After he died, she still had two children with handicaps to nurse. I have never heard anything but gratitude from her, even though her life is not easy.

This is true joy. It is not just a smile on my face or a spring in my step. Joy is a deep trust in my heavenly Father that remains even when tears run down my face and I cannot walk for pain.

It might be contradictory to say that happiness is not joy. But I believe that I can be joyful within my heart on days when I cannot truthfully say that I am happy. Happiness often depends on what is happening in my life and on circumstances that affect my emotions.

When I see a beautiful flower, it makes me happy. When I have correct change in my wallet, I am happy. When a friend calls me, it brings me happiness.

Joy is much more than that. It begins when I give my life to God. In Psalm 51:12, David prayed, "Restore unto me the joy of thy salvation." When I am saved, there is joy. When I sin, that joy leaves.

But God is faithful to forgive me when I repent and turn from sin. He restores my joy. That's a glorious promise and a beautiful gift.

Joy grows in a humble heart. Isaiah 29:19 reads that "the meek also shall increase their joy." Being humbly at peace with God, and therefore also with my family, my neighbors, and my coworkers, brings joy.

The people I love may do and say hurtful things. A humble heart that is open to God will still have joy despite the pain. Nehemiah 8:10 reminds us that "the joy of the Lord is your strength."

I want to be strong, I want to walk boldly and courageously. So I must seek his strength by first knowing his joy.

Someone once told me that I can choose what kind of day to have. In a way, that is so. When I feel disgruntled, it helps to kneel and humbly ask God to forgive me and to restore his joy to the degree that it fills my heart and reaches my face. It is also true that if I persist in filling my mind with negative thoughts, I will be anything but joyful.

Joy? On the same day you wreck a car? Highly unlikely, right? But it happened to me. In the first minutes after the crash, I stumbled around, dismayed, and yes, very unhappy. But a dear friend was soon on the scene, and we prayed together. In those moments of quietness, I realized that yes, God was there, even then. He gave me joy despite the sorrow of the accident and monetary loss. God is my joy.

prayer

Dear Lord, giver of joy, let my life reflect your joy today. Remind me that circumstances do not need to derail a heart fixed on you.

reflection

Think of someone you know who radiates joy even in difficult circumstances. Pray for that person today.

3

ALTAR OF PEACE

Isaiah 26:1-4, 12-13

*W*hen my family travels, everyone seems to enjoy staying on vacation "one day longer" except me. I have learned, for the sake of peace, to accept the majority vote. And when I find joy in submitting, it is interesting to see how often my family is willing to accommodate my wishes in other things. Like dropping me off at a bookstore while the car is refueled, even when it takes me longer than the gas pump. Like stopping at a roadside stand for fresh fruit instead of grabbing packages at the supermarket. Little things? Yes, but they bring harmony.

Is peace mainly the absence of conflict? Obviously, when there's no conflict, there is peace. But peace is much more than no conflict or disagreement.

Ephesians 2:14 gives the answer to real peace: "For he is our peace, who hath made both one, and hath broken down the middle wall of partition between us." This is referring to salvation by Christ's death on Calvary's cross. When he died there, he opened the way for us to be in God's presence. Before this time, in the Old Testament, people had to have a mediator, the high priest, who was the only one who talked with God (with the exception of a few special people whom God used).

Today, I don't have to offer animal sacrifices once yearly to absolve my sins, for my sins are washed away by the blood of the true Lamb of God, Jesus. There is nothing that brings peace like knowing that my soul is clean before God.

When I have that peace, I can also be at peace with those around me. Ephesians 4:3 speaks of "endeavouring to keep the unity of the Spirit in the bond of peace."

I understand by the word *endeavour* that keeping peace includes an effort. It's not just automatic. I have to work at it. In this chapter in Ephesians, the apostle Paul is speaking to the church. We are one in Christ, and therefore united by the Holy Spirit. Seems like peace should be simple.

Why then must I "endeavour"? Because I am still in this human body, with natural tendencies to want my own way. And that brings conflict, because I live and work with other humans who also want their own way.

When peace is shattered, I need to find where the problem is. Is it sin in my heart? Sometimes I must actively work to restore a relationship. A conscience at peace is worth the struggle and the surrender.

Recently someone shared about a conflict she had with her sister. After listening, I asked if she realized the devil might be the source of the conflict. God is peace. Satan brings grief and confusion. She was silent a long while and then said, "Yes! It is Satan. And by God's grace, the devil will not ruin my relationship with my sister." The victory is won when we listen to God's voice, not Satan's.

How do I maintain peace? By learning to live as Jesus did, in humility and love, and by sacrificing not principles, but ideas, on the altar of peace.

prayer

Lord, you are the author of peace. As such, I come to you and thank you for the peace that comes through knowing Jesus' blood has covered my sins. When I feel confused, may I turn to you for victory and for restoration of your peace.

reflection

Are there conversations you need to have to restore peace in your relationships or your conscience this week?

4

LONG-SUFFERING AND GENTLENESS

Luke 6:27-38

Some days I suffer long with those I love. I really suffer, and the day is long. That doesn't mean that I am long-suffering. Many times I am not. I suffer, but I do it loudly, impatiently, and rudely. I make sure everyone knows I am suffering.

Merriam-Webster's definition for *long-suffering* is "patiently enduring extended periods of trial and pain." That gives quite a different picture. And it's not easy to do. Perhaps I can endure anything for a day or for an hour. But for an extended time? Ouch.

And endure patiently? Doesn't that imply sweetness and cheerfulness?

Obviously the attitude of long-suffering must come from Christ's work in me. I cannot manufacture it.

It is a wonderful attribute of God. If you have a concordance or Internet access, research the term *long-suffering*. Most of the time the Bible uses it in reference to our Lord. He is long-suffering toward me. Toward you. He has amazing patience despite all our failures to live perfectly in his will. Oh, may his Spirit work in me so that I can show mercy to others.

In this grace, may I also be gentle. When I am upset and frustrated, I can still show long-suffering and gentleness toward those around me because of God's life within.

Some mornings are hectic with trying to get schoolchildren ready and lunches packed for them and all the carpenters who live at my house. Before I know it, I might be snapping at someone who dawdles—or spills the orange juice. At times, God will remind me that my attitude is wrong. His grace will help me calm down, help me to say, "I am sorry. Please forgive me." I can then send them all out the door with a smile.

To be gentle simply means extending a quiet kindness to anyone and everyone. It is never rude or thoughtless, but it lifts a burden for another. It shares an encouraging word; it shows pity for the fallen.

I have been blessed by phone calls of encouragement and reminders of prayer on weeks when we were especially busy. These are acts of mercy. I am blessed and humbled by forgiveness my loved ones show even when I mess up. The cake that flopped? They bravely choke it down. The shirt I turned pink? "It'll wash out." And a heartfelt "I forgive you" from a family member when I spoke hastily.

As a child, I remember dropping a glass measuring cup into a huge batch of cookies we were making to take to the farmers market, and watching, horrified, as the cup shattered. Mother didn't speak harshly even as we dumped the whole batch of ruined batter over the fence. Mercy? Yes.

God has shown such mercy and kindness to me—can I refuse to show gentleness to others? It is the fruit of my life when I am flourishing in his will. If I am connected with him, by obedience to the Word and by prayer, I will show long-suffering and gentleness.

prayer

Lord, your mercy is overwhelming. I am awed by your forgiveness. Thank you for putting people into my life who have shown your gentleness. May I extend mercy and long-suffering to all I meet today.

reflection

Think of someone who has shown mercy to you. Write a letter or call to say thank you.

5

"I WANT TO BE GOOD"

Romans 15:1-14

My uncle is a great example of goodness. The Lord has blessed him financially, and he shares willingly to bless others. Years ago, he paid my father's debt, as he knew dad was a busy minister and bishop with oversight of several churches, including mission churches far away. Once he provided a vehicle and an all-expenses-paid trip for missionaries on furlough. But you won't hear about these acts of goodness from him. He is also truly humble.

"I want to be good." That's a small child's prayer, but perhaps I need to pray it as well.

I have heard my neighbor describe our mechanic as being a good person. What does that mean? Possibly it's a way to say that such a person is faithful in work, honest in business, and wholesome in speech.

To be morally good is excellent. It implies purity and virtue. To be honest and virtuous is commendable. But I need more than that. I need the goodness of God in my heart. This goodness grows from knowing him and his perfect goodness.

In Psalm 118, verses 1 and 29 tell us "He is good: because his mercy endureth forever." Psalm 119:68: "Thou art good, and doest good." Many other Scriptures tell us that God is good. Praise him! I don't ever need to be afraid to let him be in control, for he is good. And all that he works in my life is good, even when it might seem as evil to me. He is good. It's that simple. And he wants to work out his good will in me.

Romans 3:12 reads: "There is none that doeth good, no, not one."

How then can I produce this fruit of the Spirit? Here's the secret: it is not me—it is God's Spirit.

On the first day that I taught school, the former teacher penned Philippians 1:6 to me: "He which hath begun a good work in you will perform it until the day of Jesus Christ." What an encouragement that was!

Christ has saved me, and he will continue to work in my life his grace, which alone makes me good. It's not a superficial "good person" quality, but a heart condition.

Titus 2 talks specifically of women, "keepers at home, good, obedient . . ." I am called to be good. Not merely good, but filled with the goodness of God.

My two sisters-in-law are excellent in their acts of goodness toward many who stop at their deli. I have seen them show patience to a tottering, elderly person and lend a listening ear to a hurting soul. They plan special menus and activities to delight their nieces and nephews. They could complain about all the work the extended family creates when they drop by, but they welcome their relatives (or visitors) because their hearts are full of God's love.

When someone says of me, "She's a good person," may it be because I have tasted that God is good and his goodness is reflected in my words and actions.

prayer

Heavenly Father, you alone are good. Any good that I may seem to do is only because of your work in my life. Today may the fruit of my heart be wholesome, pure, and good.

reflection

Are you merely good—or are you filled with God's goodness?

6

ACTIVE FAITH

James 2:14-26

A few years ago our family faced a time of testing. Finances were a fiasco, and jobs were practically nonexistent. Other stresses were slamming against us too. Our family wasn't alone; others we loved were also struggling.

Did God leave us? Absolutely not. He is there even when I can't see him or feel him. It's not so much that I have a great faith, but that I believe in a great God. My faith is settled because he is God.

Hebrews 11:6 states clearly, "But without faith it is impossible to please him: for he that cometh to God must believe that he is, and that he is a rewarder of them that diligently seek him."

My life's goal is to please God. Without believing in his existence, that goal fails. That verse says that God will reward the ones who seek him diligently. Can I believe that? Even on days when I struggle to believe that he cares, I must reach out and, if need be, cry out as the disciples did: "Lord, increase my faith."

It takes faith to pray that; it takes faith to realize that he already knows when I am floundering in despair. It's no use to try to hide my doubts. He knows about them, and what's more, he understands. Better still, he cares.

It's hard to explain why I believe. How do I describe that depth of peace in my soul? This confidence comes because I know he is God. He saved my soul, he daily delivers me from the devil and his snares. He is trustworthy and faithful.

Faith is not passive. It is actively claiming the promises of God's Word and working to live out that faith. The best evidence of true faith is my obedience to the Bible. I cannot say "I have faith" and continue to live in defeat. Faith finds victory through surrender to Christ and to his will and Word.

Faith is taking hold of those promises and finding them fulfilled. Maybe not today. Maybe the only answer I may ever know is his peace.

When we were moving from Missouri to California, a friend gave us a card with these profound words: "Faith is coming to the very end of all that I know, and taking one more step toward God." That comment challenged me to let God increase my faith as we faced many unknowns, especially as the friend who shared the encouragement was also moving.

God answered our prayers for steady work, more stability in our church, and fellowship for our children. Our friends' situation also improved. God doesn't always answer how we wish, but it is always right, because he is God.

The week my uncle Enos died, he said, "Satan wants to make it look like it's too hard for anyone to reach heaven. But I believe in the blood of Jesus." That's faith.

prayer

Lord, I believe. Strengthen my faith and give me courage to live out my faith by works that glorify you. When I reach the end of the known path, let me clasp the hand of the One who walks before me and leads me into the light.

reflection

When is your faith most tested? How can you take one more step toward God in that moment?

7

MEEKNESS AND TEMPERANCE

Philippians 2

At one gathering of church sisters, we were avidly discussing the best way to stitch the quilt, but we were not agreeing. Suddenly, I looked over at the oldest sister. She was quietly waiting for our decision so she could get busy. "You have done this pattern before. What do *you* think?" I asked, ashamed that we hadn't asked her first. Humbly, she instructed us, and we were surprised at how easily and well it worked.

At another meeting, one sister informed someone that she was taking charge of a duty that wasn't her business. The second sister only chuckled and said, "I'm sorry. I had no idea. You go right ahead." Her serene spirit reminded me of Psalm 119:165: "Great peace have they which love thy law: and nothing shall offend them." It takes great meekness to accept a scolding, especially when it's undeserved.

Meekness is submissive, humble patience in the face of injury. It isn't weakness at all, as I may think, but it shows great strength that faithfully, triumphantly endures.

It is not resentful when my wishes are disregarded, my good deeds are ignored, and my skills overlooked. It is strength harnessed by God's grace.

When I feel overburdened by another's demands, meekness doesn't just sit there like a doormat. It takes a huge dose of meekness to humbly address an issue rather than to suffer and seethe. Christ talked about things that troubled him, and he wants us to work through situations we encounter rather than stumble over them or skirt around them.

"Blessed are the meek: for they shall inherit the earth" (Matthew 5:5). God places great value on a humble heart. Humility is active, not passive. The Bible instructs us to "Humble yourselves" (1 Peter 5:6). It takes a heart that recognizes who God is and who I am in him. His holiness is so pure, his person so almighty, that one honest look at him brings me to my knees in awe and humility.

Meekness seeks moderation, which is another form of temperance.

Temperance denotes a balanced life. Not too busy, too relaxed, too tired, too sleep-saturated, too full, too hungry, too bouncy, too lethargic. Just guided by a calm, ordered spirit no matter what comes, which proves that the Holy Spirit reigns.

It's not thinking that if one pot of coffee perks me up, three will energize me. Or that one day of shopping is therapeutic, so five days will be perfect. Coffee's fine and shopping must be done. But all things must be tempered by moderation.

Can I be too joyful? Too filled with the Spirit? Too holy?

Probably not. If I am so connected to God that his life is real and vibrant within me, I will be moderate in everything. Even in prayer and Bible study. Most of us will never have too much of that, but a life spent in the locked back bedroom, praying and studying the Bible, is not a fruitful life. Sometime I must enter the world and live out the lessons God is teaching me. I learn best by doing.

His life within me produces fruit that brings honor to his holy name.

prayer

May your Spirit, O holy God, be within me, directing my thoughts, words, and actions. I long to produce fruit that glorifies you and blesses others. Only through you is it possible. Help me to stay close to you, for you are my life.

reflection

When is weakness a substitute for meekness? How can you show a positive meek strength today? In what area do you struggle to be temperate?

1

THE MIGHTY SEA

Psalm 95

The first time I saw the ocean, I stood in awe—and the second
time, the third, and each time since. I can never get enough of
that part of God's awesome creation.

There is so much water, so much power. Seventy percent of the
earth's surface is water. What vastness! Does the ocean never tire?
All that ebb and flow, the constant pull and push? We can only see a
tiny portion, but it's enough to cause us to marvel at its vast power
and depth.

Several years ago we were privileged to travel to Sarasota, Florida. We were eager to see the Gulf of Mexico and compare it to the
Pacific. The calm, blue waters off Florida mirrored the azure skies.
Gleaming white sand made it picture-perfect. Stately palms and
elegant beach houses bordered the water. The water temperature was
much warmer than the northern Pacific. Even in March, we waded
in waist-deep, looking for sand dollars and other seashells. "This is
a different ocean!" I told my husband. "I love the temperature but I
miss the pounding waves."

His grin told me he enjoyed it too.

The allure of the sea is indescribable. Even when we don't dash
into its depths, we are drawn to at least get our feet wet. There's something about the vast ocean that calls to one's deepest being. Standing
there, gazing at the water that touches Japan on the other side, one
can only recognize God and his majesty. We are such a small part of
his creation, yet he cares about us too.

My sister-in-law faced a time of loneliness and indecision. Where
should she go to find fellowship? What work could she do to

provide a stable income? The future looked like a wide, uncrossable ocean. She sought God's wisdom, and in time he revealed his will and gave her the idea for a business she could operate close to home. Now I see her fulfilled, contented, and enjoying precious friendships with neighbors who come to her store. God provided a way for her through the ocean of perplexity and desolation.

God is master of every situation, and I too can face my ocean with courage.

"O come, let us worship and bow down: let us kneel before the Lord our maker," says Psalm 95:6. I stand in joy and awe.

prayer

Dear Lord, creator of the sea, thank you for making the world at your command. Thank you for being master of the ocean and also for caring about tiny me, with my daily problems and cares.

reflection

What problem is staring at you today? Can you embrace God's power and release everything to him?

2

POWERFUL,
YET PEACEFUL

Psalm 98

The northern coast of California is ruggedly beautiful. The sand is not white, but dirty gray, littered with bleached driftwood smooth from washing in the ocean's depths. Enormous boulders with jagged edges and massive height tower over the sea. The waters crash against the rocks, showering sprays of water high into the sky.

Seldom is the sea calm. The waves keep coming, splashing and crashing thunderously against the shore. We love it! Just to sit beside the water, listening to the roar, watching the white spray showering the beach, and marveling at our great God, is therapeutic.

The name Pacific means "peaceful," but that's hardly the correct word to describe "our" shoreline. Portuguese explorer Ferdinand Magellan named it. He sailed the sea for weeks, driven by peaceful winds, but obviously the name is sometimes a misnomer.

My brother-in-law, whose family camped with us along the coast, walked along the sand for a distance. When he returned he said in awe, "If the ocean doesn't make one think of God, something is wrong. Only God could create such a marvel."

They were facing a life-changing move and possibly the end of financial security. But with their gaze focused on the God who created the ocean, the God who governs the world, they knew he would also guide them in the uncertainties of the future.

The ocean's power thrills me too. As I view the strength of the sea and the force of the mighty waves, the troubles I face seem to diminish. All the trials that distress me, all the difficulties that seem like mountains, and all the shadows that darken the joy in my heart cannot possibly be too hard for God. After an hour of watching the waves, my heart feels washed clean like the rocks that glisten in the evening light.

"O Lord, how manifold are thy works! in wisdom hast thou made them all: the earth is full of thy riches. So is this great and wide sea, wherein are things creeping innumerable, both small and great beasts. There go the ships . . ." (Psalm 104:24-26).

It's so big and wide and powerful. But it gives us just a little glimpse of the almighty power of our great and awesome God.

prayer

Heavenly Father, I give to you all the problems and cares I face. Take complete control, just as you do of the ocean. And send to me a great calm.

reflection

Do you believe that God can calm the storm in your life? Will you today seek to keep your heart at peace?

3

STORMY SEAS

Acts 27:9-24

The Pacific Ocean is the largest body of water in the world. All the continents could fit inside this ocean, with space left for another Asia. What a marvelous God, to create such vast bodies of water. No wonder the sea is powerful.

The psalmist says, "They that go down to the sea in ships, that do business in great waters; These see the works of the Lord, and his wonders in the deep" (Psalm 107:23-24).

Those that make their livelihood on the ocean, or near it, learn to respect its strength or be lost by it. Even in this day of technology that keeps oceangoing vessels safe, lighthouses beckon to warn sailors whose smaller crafts may crash against the shore, and foghorns bellow out their mournful call.

We've all heard about terrible crashes along the shore, when sudden storms appear and the ship captain is unprepared. This was the case in today's Scripture reading.

The apostle Paul, a prisoner, was being taken to another country. He told the captain that it wasn't a good time to sail, but his words were scoffed and ignored—until the winds began to blow and the ship began to toss. I wonder if the captain remembered Paul's warning then. But it was far too late to change course.

The verses tell of turmoil, and through it all we sense the fear that grasped the hearts of those aboard. All but Paul. His heart was calm. He knew God ruled the sea, and God is bigger than the sea. He was so close to the Lord that he knew what God wanted them to do next. This time the captain listened.

It seems like an impossibility for all those people to safely reach shore. But God is the master of the impossible. Getting the people to dry land was easy for God. He created the sea and he is also able to control it.

Sometimes he calms the storm for me. The job offer comes through, the sick child is suddenly healed, I find the missing library book. Other times he lets the storm rage and calms my heart. Once my husband and I missed a flight and I was tempted to be frustrated at the hours wasted sitting in an airport. But through prayer and committing my day to God, his tranquility brought peace, and we actually enjoyed the day. This wasn't much of a storm, perhaps, but it was a miracle to me.

prayer

Lord, I don't know how to ride out the storm, but you do. Teach me to cling to you, to obey you, and hold fast to the Anchor, which is Christ.

reflection

You might face an unexpected storm today. How will you respond?

4

FLOODS WON'T DROWN US

Isaiah 43:1-7

Along the shore of the Pacific Ocean stand huge rocks. Beaten by thousands of years of waves, they have withstood tremendous power. They don't flinch, they don't even shiver. They just stand there. Seagulls alight on the rocks and sway in the tempest. But their feet are on solid ground, so they are unafraid.

God is my rock. He is unmovable, unchangeable, and unshakeable. I can safely stand on his love, his mercy, and his promises. He won't let me fall. I can also face the storms of life unafraid.

Even while natural rocks may eventually give up the battle and shift or tumble, God will not. He has promised to be here for me, no matter what, no matter where. He is bigger than the storm, bigger than the waves. Bigger even than a tsunami.

Have you come to a deep-sea place in your life? Maybe you're looking across a vast unknown, and not only is it vast but it is stormy and dark. The waves go out and you think the sea is growing calm, but then the waves come crashing back.

I've been there. During a particularly hard time in my life, I felt my confidence waning with each new wave. I was tempted to forget trying to master the waves. I wanted to let go and drown. But, by God's grace, instead of throwing myself into the waves, I stood on the Rock.

A dear friend lost her husband of fifty-one years. She has a hard time coping with a quiet house and lonely hours. Some days she is tempted to quit trying to be strong. It's easier to drown in the waves of grief than to trust God. But day by desolate day, she is learning to release her pain and sorrow and to joyfully stand on the Rock who never lets her go.

How awesome is our God! How much he loves me! His love transcends the depth of the ocean, the width of the sea. I can trust God with all confidence. His power, which controls the sea, will also work in my life to bring order to the chaos that threatens to crash me against the shore of defeat.

Because of his great love, God longs for me to experience his power. This doesn't mean I am not frightened by waves of conflict, despair, and pain. It does mean that I can learn to cling to him even in the middle of the storm.

prayer

Lord, I don't want to drown. I want to feel your presence as a rock beneath my feet, and as a peace to my fearful soul. Keep me standing on the Rock.

reflection

How will you react the next time your life seems chaotic?

5

A LITTLE SEA, A BIG GOD

Mark 4:1, 34-41

*H*ave you ever set out on a boat ride when the water was calm, only to have a storm blow up and frighten you? In today's reading, Jesus and his disciples were on the Sea of Galilee. It's not uncommon there for sudden storms to blow up without much warning.

Jesus had preached to the multitudes, no doubt for hours. He was tired, so he slept. He is also God of the sea, so he kept right on sleeping even during a tempestuous storm. When awakened, his command to the waves calmed the storm. It was a little thing to the Creator.

A long look at the ocean reminds us of God. He isn't only a God of big things. He is also a God of the little things. Even so, the things that storm into my life are small to him. He isn't worried or dismayed. And yet he cares about my tumultuous heart. For the God who controls the tides, the waves, and the climate also cares for the tiny plankton swimming in the ocean and the tiny bugs that feed on washed-up seaweed.

In the daily round of duties, when the bills keep coming and the paycheck doesn't reach, when relationships with friends seem to have soured and the close comradeship once shared seems lost, when even those dearest to me don't understand, when my physical strength doesn't last for the long day and my workload magnifies before my eyes, I must remember God.

The God who created the sea cares for the seagull, and he cares for me. This isn't just a trite saying, something that gives me a warm-fuzzy feeling of peace. Rather, it is a deep-seated trust in my heavenly Father, a confident reaching for his hand when the way looks dark. It is fervently searching the Word for answers to those problems that plague. It is rising each morning with courage, and all through the day doing the next thing that needs to be done. It is kneeling down at night in peace, having my sins washed away by the precious blood of Jesus. It is placing on his shoulders the burdens I tend to carry long after I should have relinquished them to his power. It is sleeping soundly, in hope of the eternal rest that awaits.

"Then they cried unto the Lord in their trouble, and he saved them out of their distresses. . . . Oh that men would praise the Lord for his goodness, and for his wonderful works to the children of men!" (Psalm 107:13, 15). No matter what I face, he is with me "in the boat." His presence brings calm to my soul.

prayer

Lord, I am sorry for failing to trust you. Increase my faith, and show me how to rest in you in the midst of the storm.

reflection

How will you respond when the waves hit? What will you do to keep your spirit calm when your boat starts rocking?

6

WALK, SINK, OR SWIM

John 14:22-33

I have watched people surfing and swimming, and I marvel. I would love to join them—it looks so easy. But from past experience, I know I would simply sink. As it is, I can wade a little or board a ship to ride the waves.

But what if there were no boats to carry one across? How could I cross the water?

Sometimes I come to places in my life that look as impossible to cross as the ocean.

Today's Scripture passage challenges me. Maybe I, like Peter, can walk on top of the sea. It seems to me that Jesus was showing the disciples that they had a choice. They could cower, absolutely terrified by the storm, or they could walk to Jesus. Boldly, courageously, trustingly.

Peter's walk went well—until he looked around him and noticed that the waves were still pounding.

As soon as I take my eyes off Jesus, I too will go under.

Physically, if I went under, I would drown. But spiritually, even when the waves are over my head, I can cling to the One who holds me up.

It takes a complete trust in God, who holds the waves in his hand. I want to learn to swim through trials. It brings me confidence to remember that even when the waves are over my head, they are still under his feet.

He promises that the waters won't overwhelm, which simply means that there will be deep waters to cross, but I won't have to drown in them.

My cousin's testimony challenges me. He lost his father a few years ago and now his mother has been diagnosed with a terminal illness. Yet he says, "We're facing each day with a renewed thanks for God's grace and the time we do have with Mom. We're not swimming in grief; we're walking in faith because God is our strength." He refuses to drown in despair.

In watching his faith, my own is strengthened. My ocean suddenly looks less deep, less stormy.

I may never learn to swim in natural water. That's okay. Swimming is not mandatory, although, because of safety issues, it is a definite advantage. But in my walk with God, even during the storms, it is imperative to do more than simply succumb to the water. He reminds me to be of good cheer and to trust him completely. He will be there to lift me out of the waves and into a lasting calm.

I can choose to drown in a sea of difficulties, mistakes, or outright sin. Or I can swim through the storm courageously, knowing that on the other side there is victory. I can walk boldly, with my eyes on him and my faith rooted in him as my anchor.

prayer

Lord and Maker of the sea, teach me to keep my eyes on you and to walk upright across the waves, or to swim with courage. Above all, help me never to give up and drown.

reflection

Choices will face you today. What will you do to swim through a difficulty? How could you walk boldly? What will you do to keep from drowning in despair?

7

AM I AS
A LIGHTHOUSE
BESIDE THE SEA?

Matthew 5:13-16

The Bible doesn't speak of lighthouses or foghorns. But lighthouses have been in use for thousands of years. During the reign of Ptolemy II (283–246 BC), ancient Egyptians built the tallest lighthouse ever constructed. Over four hundred feet high, it has guided ships for about fifteen hundred years.

Before the advent of electronic navigation aids, lighthouses were designed to give off distinctive light patterns, and mariners carried a light list so they could match the light to the proper lighthouse and know where they were. Today, lighthouses are no longer as important as they once were. Still, they stand as beacons of hope and safety for those who might be floundering in the depths of the sea.

I think of the many times God's light blazed brightly to guide me. Sometimes it seemed as if the light was obscured by dense fog, but the closer I clung to him and his Word, the clearer the light shone.

Sometimes the light doesn't seem bright at all. There are several steps to follow to know God's will. First, does the thing I want to do follow the principles in the Word? Second, have I fasted and prayed? Third, have I asked counsel of strong Christians I admire?

If I still don't know which path to take, I step out in faith with one of the choices. God will either give me peace, proving it was the right decision, or he will bring more unrest, showing he wants me to choose another path.

I thank God for faithful Christians who have shown their lights to help me during times of storm and fog. They are truly following Jesus' teaching in Matthew 5 and letting their lights shine. It does no good to keep a candle under a bucket. Even so, may I show God's light and love to those I meet.

Being Mennonites, we dress distinctively. In our church affiliation, ladies wear modest cape dresses, with long skirts, and we cover our hair with a prayer covering. Menfolk have neat haircuts and groomed beards; they wear button-down shirts and suspenders. But I like to think that our faces and actions also speak distinctively of God.

Once when our family was in San Francisco, a police officer stopped us to visit. He asked if he could snap a photograph of us and said, "I see so much trouble and despair; your family caught my attention immediately. In the midst of the wicked city, you stand out as messengers of peace."

My husband assured him that it is because of the life of Jesus within. He is our light and he will shine through us.

prayer

Dear Lord, thank you for being my light. May I shine your light to those around me, so that those in troubled waters may find safety in your harbor.

reflection

What can you do today that shines God's light to everyone you meet?

1

A HOSPITABLE HEART

2 Kings 4:8-17

*M*y cousin reminds me of the Shunammite woman in the book of 2 Kings. The Bible calls her a great woman. My cousin's guest bedroom has a bed, a chair, a table, and a lamp. There are even extras: a pitcher of ice water and cups, with a few chocolates nestled beside them.

Another friend's guest room is filled with freshly cut flowers, fluffy towels, a sweet note, and a tray of snacks. Still another has a basket of magazines, extra blankets, and pillows.

Once, an early morning knock at the door revealed a little girl holding a tray of steaming coffee. Her mother, my sister, knew I love to awaken to coffee and she cared enough to make it happen.

And speaking of coffee—my sister-in-law serves it in delicate china cups. She brews it for me whenever I'm nearby, and I am touched by her effort and consideration. There's something about visiting over steaming cups that opens our hearts to share.

Another sister models my aunt. They are both known to arise early to prepare fresh snacks for our journey homeward. Sweet, gooey crispy rice bars warm the heart all the way home.

Helping guests feel welcome is a gift I can cultivate as well. I don't remember all the meals hosts have fed us or all the cozy accommodations. But I am still blessed by the love that fixed the meals and the time they sacrificed to spend with us.

Once we slept in our own guest room—and good thing! The mattress was hard and the pillows were lumpy. We decided to try all the mattresses and replace the uncomfortable ones. It's also good to have different styles of pillows, as preferences vary. Having a reading lamp is a simple but thoughtful addition, as is a chair. Back when I had nursing babies, sometimes I ended up sitting on the floor to feed them.

Hospitality is thinking of others and doing what we can to make them feel at home. A caring, welcoming heart is the best gift a host can offer. Add to that a sincere smile and a restful spirit, and your guest will be thankful to be at your house.

Proverbs 11:25 is an encouragement. Be a blessing, and you will be blessed! Don't try to make an impression or to be opulent in your hospitality. It's not about putting on a show or gathering compliments. It's about showing God's love to friend or stranger.

Even if my house isn't the tidiest and I'm in the middle of a baking session, if my heart is filled with God's love I will welcome a visitor who comes, without stammering out a paragraph of apologies. My sister is an excellent example in this, and I am learning to be more hospitable, whether or not the visit was preplanned.

When I do know company is coming, it makes my day run more smoothly if I start preparations as early as possible. If I have even ten minutes to sit before visitors arrive, my spirit is more prepared to welcome them. I pray for my heart to be always filled with God's love, so that no matter when I have the privilege to entertain company, they will feel God's welcoming grace in my smile.

prayer

Father, many people have given me shelter. Help me to cultivate a loving heart so that others may find a welcome in my home.

reflection

Is company a drain or a blessing? How can you show hospitality in Christ's love?

2

A HEART
LIKE DORCAS'

Acts 9:36-42

I read with awe the few verses that summarize the life of Dorcas. Wouldn't it be a blessing to have such an amazing testimony? My aunt reminds me of Dorcas. I remember a few times when we got to her house at a late hour. She wouldn't let us go to bed without feeding us. Those peanut butter and pickle sandwiches make my mouth water even now.

My aunt didn't have a richly furnished house. But it was filled with love and laughter. She had the gift of making us feel welcome and special. Even a bed in the basement was sweet because of her touch. She would race out to pick peas for us because she knew they were our favorite. She popped popcorn until we had eaten our fill. She is a Dorcas.

When Dorcas died, people wept bitterly. With great agony they showed Peter the garments she had lovingly stitched. Their appeal to him touched his heart, as well as their obvious love and regard for Dorcas.

I think they were weeping not merely because a skillful seamstress was gone, but also because she loved them. The verses say she did good works and gave alms. Giving alms is not only dropping a few dollars into the offering plate at church. It also includes acts of mercy, of sharing money, food, and clothes with the poor. Giving to the needy is an act of mercy all its own because we are not expecting any return.

When my children were young, I often felt I could do little for others outside my family. God understands. He does not require me to give what I cannot. In those years, time was a commodity I could scarcely give, but as the years passed and the children grew, time was more abundant. My mother felt the same way, and since there were six girls in our family, she often sent us to help when she couldn't go.

When finances are stretched to the max, it doesn't seem prudent to give more money than we have to the poor. Or perhaps we hardly have enough clothes to go around. What then?

What did I have to give? I longed to give, for we had received so much from our Lord. As I sought God through prayer and study of the Word, he showed me that everyone has something to give.

While my sister purchased items to send to missionaries, I wrote letters. While my aunt sewed dozens of little dresses to send overseas, I took my children to sing for a lonely widow. Did my lowly deeds count as much for alms as that of the others? God knows. If I serve with love, alert to the needs I can meet, they are almsdeeds of mercy, and God is glorified. Second Corinthians 9 says that we are judged not by what we do, but by our motives. God blesses our willingness.

I love the ending of Acts 9. When God raised Dorcas from her dead slumber, "many believed in the Lord" (verse 42). Isn't that why I serve with mercy? To show God's love.

prayer

Dear God, thank you for the testimony of Dorcas. Open my eyes to the needs of others, and show me how best to show your love in acts of mercy. My time, money, and possessions are yours. May I use them to bless others.

reflection

Will you be remembered for acts of kindness? Pray for God to show you what to give this week.

3

PASSING ON
THE FAITH

2 Timothy 1:1-5

My father and his brothers cannot speak about their mother without tears. They unabashedly call her a saint. Grandma died before I was born, and I have longed to know her. Her faith obviously translated into love for her seventeen children, and she taught godly principles. Out of the seven sons who grew to adulthood, five were ministers of the gospel.

They tell of Sunday afternoons when Grandma read aloud from the Bible. They talk of her pleading with tears when they wanted to leave for town late at night. They speak of prayers uttered with groaning, and a spirit that yearned after her wayward sons.

But their honor and regard for Grandma would mean little if they were not also following her God and embracing the faith she exemplified. I too long to continue in the faith of my heritage.

Timothy was a young man who apparently had no godly father or grandfather. Apostle Paul, in addressing him with affection, recalls the pure and holy faith that his grandmother Lois had. She taught her daughter Eunice, who in turn taught Timothy.

Paul was convinced that Timothy had embraced the faith of his mother and grandmother. But it takes more than a celebration of their faith; it takes an adherence to it.

By God's help, we want to pass our faith to our children, who I pray will then guide their children in the same faith. Verses in Deuteronomy 6 give me positive direction. They don't list a lot of what not to do, but say simply to teach the Word and the fear of the Lord.

Teach it by living it out. Teach it by talking about God when we're on a walk, in the car, around the table.

Have Bible verses printed on sticky notes on the mirror. Recite Scripture while you're washing dishes. When the children have memory verses to learn at school or Sunday school, count it a joy to help them.

Some of our children learned Psalm 23 on the way to school. Every morning I recited it, and they joined in where they could until they had memorized it. A simple thing, yet it has lasting value. The more their minds are filled with God, the less room there is for the devil to plant his seeds of evil. God will bring those verses to memory at the very time my children need them.

Sing about God. A song of praise to our Lord fills any day with joy. Learning songs about God is a good way to strengthen faith in myself and in my children.

Little things perhaps, but they count for much. Mothers who take this calling seriously are needed.

prayer

Father of my father and my grandmother, thank you for a heritage of faith. Thank you that even for those who have not had this heritage, they can today begin to be that heritage for their children. Grant that we may not only celebrate it but also live it.

reflection

Have you thanked your mother or grandmother for all they taught you? What legacy are you leaving for your children?

4

A BRAVE MOTHER

Exodus 2:1-10; Hebrews 11:23

*M*y sister's friend was ecstatic. She didn't get married until she was middle-aged, and now she was expecting her first child! But oh—what pain struck her heart when a test showed that the baby had Down syndrome. The doctor suggested she abort the baby. She cried to my sister, who encouraged her to choose life for the unborn child. The diagnosis was incorrect, but even if it had not been, our friend's faith was growing, and no matter what happened, the baby would be accepted with love. Whether the test was false or whether God healed the baby doesn't matter. What matters is her faith and that she acted on that faith.

I also marvel at the faith of a mother who crafted a little boat out of grasses and pitch, and placed her baby within, and then set it to float on the river. What a brave woman!

Hebrews 11:23 says that Jochabed, Moses's mother, and her husband weren't afraid even though the king had ordered all infant sons to be killed. The midwives in those days were also gallant. They had been commanded to kill all the baby boys as they were delivered.

"But the midwives feared God, and did not as the king of Egypt commanded them, but saved the men children alive" (Exodus 1:17). If they had not feared God, there would have been no Moses to talk about. But God was ruling in the lives of his people, and we are thankful for the midwives who feared God more than they feared the king, even at the risk of their lives.

Jochabed saw that Moses was a goodly child and decided to hide him as long as possible. God apparently kept Moses from getting colic or other ailments, because Jochabed hid him for three months.

Her next step must have been taken in complete faith. I wonder if she knew the habits of the princess and purposely placed the baby where the princess would find him. What a risk Jochabed took! The princess was a daughter to the king who had ordered all boys to be killed. She could have thrown Moses into the river with no qualms.

But God was also working in the princess's heart. He appealed to the love we have for babies and moved her to save Moses. If the king had known his grandson (the Bible says Moses became the princess's son) would grow to be a deliverer of the people, can you imagine his wrath? But God was in control. Because people all along the path of Moses's life had chosen to obey God above the king's wicked order, God worked out his plan and purpose for the multitudes of Hebrews.

Fifty-some years ago, an Amish man was briefly imprisoned because he refused to obey an order that he thought was against the Word of God. At that time children were all sent to public schools and on to high school. This man saw the effects of worldly teachings on his children, and he respectfully requested to remove them from school after eight years.

Because he feared God more than the authorities, others appealed to the higher courts regarding his request. New laws were formed, and Amish schools were exempted from following the standards for public schools. To this day, we reap benefits regarding educational freedoms from this one man's faith and courage. Could I stand alone if it meant imprisonment or death?

prayer

Dear Lord, thank you for the examples of those who truly lived their faith, who obeyed you above all. Grant that I may always live by the Word and fear of God, and when I am required to do something that does not follow those principles, fill me with courage to obey you.

reflection

In what way can you show that you are a person who fears God?

5

PRISCILLA'S GIFT OF GRACE

Acts 18:1-3, 18, 24-28; Romans 16:3-4

My father was a minister, and many were the deeds of love we received as a family. I recall finding groceries or baked goods in our car, a woodpile restocked, a vehicle loaned, a bill paid. As children sometimes we cringed at all that people did for us, wishing we could do more for them. We vowed that with God's help we would do the same for other ministers, when we were grown. May I renew that zeal to especially bless those who are laboring for God in preaching the Word.

It's a blessing to show special kindnesses to a family whose father is preaching away from home. It doesn't have to be a great thing, but even a bouquet of flowers lets them know we are thinking of them during a lonely week.

The apostle Paul was often in trouble with the authorities because of boldly preaching the word of God. But there were also years of relative peace for Paul, and during some of those he lived with friends, Aquila and his wife, Priscilla. Paul shared a similar craft, making tents. That may have been the first reason Paul moved in with them, but other verses show how much they encouraged him in his work and faith.

The latter part of Acts 18 talks about how they helped another disciple to learn the word of God more perfectly. Apollos was fervent in serving God and open to what Aquila and Priscilla taught him. He went on to be an effective minister for God. It couldn't have been easy for Aquila and Priscilla to exhort a preacher, but they obeyed the promptings of the Holy Spirit, and God blessed that.

First Corinthians 16:19 makes reference to Aquila and Priscilla and "the church that is in their house." I wonder if that meant they hosted church services, or if all their household was in such service to God that their house was like a church of its own. Either way, they were steadfast in spreading the gospel by hospitality and kindness.

When we moved here, church services were held at our minister's shop for nearly five years. It couldn't have always been convenient, and no doubt their family schedule was often interrupted, especially when school was also conducted there. May God reward them for this sacrifice.

The verses in Romans 16 show the great love Paul had for Aquila and Priscilla. He calls them his helpers in Christ, and says that they had laid down their lives for his sake. What commitment!

Obviously Priscilla stood with her husband in all his work and exhortation. They weren't in the limelight; they didn't hold high offices. They simply did all that they could to further the gospel of the kingdom, starting with kindness to Paul.

In a later epistle (2 Timothy 4:19), Paul remembers them and asks Timothy to salute them. Because of their love for the Lord, their gracious love to him would be a testimony for all time.

prayer

Heavenly Father, may I be a Priscilla today. Help me to reach out to ease a burden for another, and to aid those who are serving others. In simple ways I want to show your love to those who are your ministers.

reflection

How can you show respect and kindness toward a missionary or a minister today?

6

PHEBE'S
FAITHFULNESS

Romans 16:1-2; James 2:14-26

*M*y friend's aunt is a faithful example of service and sacrifice. Her life mirrors the work of God. She opened her home to countless foster children and has adopted two. Now she is practically raising her grandson. For years she cared for her grandparents, then for her aging parents, down to the not-so-lovely toilet and bathing duties. Unselfishly she gave up her freedom and privacy to move them into her house. When they struggled with thoughts of dying, she prayed with them and encouraged them until they were excited about going "home." She showed her love in countless, tireless ways, asking for nothing but the approval of God.

I think she might feel a bit like the Phebe we read about in Romans 16. Just a few verses to summarize a life, but they speak eloquently of the beauty of service and sacrifice. I am filled with admiration for Phebe and for my friend's aunt. I long to, like them, unselfishly serve others.

I appreciate the apostle Paul's commendation of Phebe, and also his plea that others would help her in whatever way they could. Sometimes I think that women aren't honored as they could or should be, but here is a clear picture of Paul praising a faithful servant of Christ.

Paul didn't leave room for others to censure her; maybe she was helping someone who should have been helping himself, or maybe her fruit basket could have been sent to a worthier place. No,

Paul just said they should assist her in all the business she needed help with.

I find that it can be a challenge to be supportive of others' ministries without coming up with a host of better ideas. Just to simply help them as they help others. It frees my mind to simply serve, and it frees their schedule to help even more people.

Paul ends that little note of respect by saying that Phebe was a support to many and also an aid to him. That denotes an unselfish giving of time or money.

I may not be a Phebe or, like my friend's aunt, one who succors many, but surely I could be of service to the one who does. That may mean serving behind the scenes. Obviously, others were helping Phebe, but their names aren't listed. Does that mean they weren't important to the work of the Lord? Absolutely not.

God sees much and also the little. If he notices a sparrow fall (and he does, according to Matthew 10:29), he certainly observes his daughters and the work they do.

Praying for others who are laboring for God is a great work and too often neglected. Maybe I say a brief "God bless them," but to earnestly intercede for them takes time and effort. But it brings a blessing to me and it certainly blesses those for whom I pray. James 5:16 clearly states that "the effectual fervent prayer of a righteous man availeth much."

Sometimes it means leaving the work I had planned for the day to join others who are cleaning a widower's house. It could be dropping a day scheduled for shopping to help the lady in charge of the sewing circle prepare blankets. No matter what it is, it matters to God.

prayer

Dear Lord, I aspire to be a Phebe, to succor many, and to do service for you. If I cannot do that, let me help other Phebes and join them in support, work, and prayer.

reflection

Do you know someone who is unselfishly serving others? How can you help her or him this week?

7

A MINISTERING HEART

Mark 1:30-31; Titus 2:1-8

There isn't much written about Peter's mother-in-law. She was deathly ill, and when she was healed, she didn't insist on being cared for tenderly. She didn't say, "I was on the brink of death, I had better take it easy for a few days. Where's my pillow? A glass of cold water? How about a foot rub?"

Instead, Mark 1:31 says, "She ministered unto them." She was so sick, and minutes later she was serving others? Somehow I think her life was a study in servanthood. It was her nature to minister. She didn't even think it was unusual to be serving others as soon as she arose from the sickbed.

Years ago I heard someone request prayer that she would be more sensitive to others and their needs. I was shocked. She was already serving in many ways. I positively hate getting meat ready for the freezer, but this sister and her family not only opened their garage for us to cut up our beef but also helped us. She was organized, and I felt blessed to be on the food committee with her. Sometimes at fellowship dinners we would quickly see that the crowd outnumbered our resources. She would pull out the homemade noodles, canned chicken, green beans, applesauce, and ice cream she had brought "for emergencies."

Could servanthood come to be second nature to me? I pray God would help me be more alert to others' needs. He answers a sincere prayer, and he shows me how to care.

I have learned much from others. If a family is planning a trip, offer to babysit while the parents pack; fix a basket of travel snacks and games; have a hot meal ready or a loaf of bread for their return. If they're gone for a while, call them. It's heartwarming to hear that one is missed.

When families have a hectic week, offer to give their children a ride to and from school to relieve their schedule. One friend invariably brought us a basket of goodies whenever she heard someone was sick.

It can be such a simple thing. Giving even one loaf of bread from each batch I bake has the possibility to bless many. Years ago when I was trying to teach my restless son to sit still, a friend slipped a note of encouragement into my Bible. Over the years I have nearly worn out that little note, but it still reminds me to keep on.

Peter's wife's mother was a lovely example for any mother-in-law. And in Titus 2, we have a beautiful picture of how older sisters-in-Christ are to teach the younger ones. I am greatly privileged to have a dear mother-in-law with whom I can share freely. She respects my ideas and I respect her years of wisdom and experience.

I am also blessed to have a few friends who were like mothers to me. I cherish their little bits of teaching thrown into our conversations, and especially their openness to share with me kindly even when it is something I didn't particularly wish to hear.

It's interesting to me to note that Titus doesn't say how the younger ladies should respond. Obviously he assumes it is with gratitude and respect and openness.

prayer

Dear Lord, thank you for all that my mother, my mother-in-law, and my other mentors have taught me, and the blessing they have been to me. Keep me open to learn from them. I want to be a woman who serves you lavishly and serves others the same way.

reflection

If you have one, how can you show your mother-in-law that you respect her? Thank the older women in your life sometime soon!

1

CONTENT WITH BEAN SOUP

Exodus 16:11-18, 31

I grew up having bean soup on winter evenings. I had difficulty swallowing it but had little choice as it was the main dish. Mom cooked navy beans, added milk, and when it was hot she crumbled bread into the soup. The result? Soggy bread. Even the browned butter she drizzled on top didn't alleviate the misery of eating hot soggy bread.

The traditions of my parents' generation included bean soup after a Sunday morning Amish church service. The accompanying cold sandwiches, unique in their own way, are still tasty in my memory and in real life. Slather peanut butter spread (corn syrup and marshmallow cream stirred into plain peanut butter until light and creamy) on a thick slab of bread, add slices of bologna and cheese, and top it with sweet pickles. Absolutely delightful.

But I vowed to save my family from the bean soup. I did pretty well until one February when I decided to make it a "Buy Few Groceries Month." We would use up our stored canned and frozen foods and buy only milk and lettuce. In a distant past I had purchased unusual items that promised to shake up a menu, so the experiment worked to clear the pantry and freezer.

As I sorted cans and found recipes to match, I wondered why I wasn't like my sister, contented with ten basic menus. But no, I wanted delectable Danish and five-step chicken parmigiana.

Now I was regretting my craving for exotic dishes. Take the bag of assorted legumes. What was I thinking when I bought it? I couldn't bare to scrap it, so I added tomato sauce and spices, but it was still only slightly palatable. I looked around at the forlorn faces of my still-hungry children and to my mind sprang the disliked soggy-bread bean soup of my childhood. I laughed then got up and fixed grilled cheese sandwiches.

It's not that we don't like soup. We do, but broccoli cheese, hearty hamburger, taco, or ham chowder. I wonder, could we learn to be content with bean soup? Or do we have to have the special, cheesy kinds to be happy?

It isn't a surprise that the children of Israel grew weary of their manna. Day in and day out, the menu was the same. Manna. They failed to realize that it was a miracle food. Perfect in every way.

God offers variety. One look at flowers and trees shows that part of God's nature. As another example, I appreciate my sister-in-law's way of planning activities to bless her nieces and nephews. In this way she is using her gifts to add variety to their lives.

Sometimes, however, life is plain and maybe even as boring as bean soup. But God offers spiritual manna: salvation, peace, and joy to the soul who seeks him. When God's love fills my heart, even the mundane tedious tasks are palatable. My task may still be to wash dishes, weed a garden, mend a shirt, or scrub a rug. But if the Lord's joy is in my heart, I can sing praises as I work, and my spirit may be content. Yes, even with bean soup.

prayer

Lord, your life within and around me keeps life interesting and joyful. When I feel bored or dull, help me to reach out for your words of inspiration and life.

reflection

Does life feel flavorless and boring? How can you add a smidgen of spice?

2

BUT I WANTED
RYE BREAD

Philemon

y aunt ordered rye toast at a café, but when it came, light-colored and soft rather than dense, she complained to the server. "I ordered rye bread. This does not look like rye."

The server said she would check to make sure it was rye. After she left, my aunt bit into the toast. "It tastes like rye bread," she admitted. When the server returned, a confused look on her face, my aunt waved her hand generously. "You're right, it is rye. It must have turned into rye when you left," she said, and started to chuckle before apologizing sincerely, to the relief of the waitress.

Once I was in the garden looking at a big green orb. Watermelon, surely. My mouth salivated at the thought. But just as I snapped off the stem, I stopped short. Watermelon stems are not thick and tough. What had I done? Plucked a very unripe pumpkin. How disappointing. I cooked the pumpkin and turned it into a squash casserole, which was delicious, but it certainly wasn't the watermelon I craved.

How do I react when things or people do not meet my expectations? I want situations to turn out a certain way. I appreciate when my children behave. I like when other people act in a way I think is correct. But situations are often beyond my control. Children and people will disappoint and embarrass me.

In today's Scripture reading, Paul was pleading for Philemon's understanding and forgiveness on behalf of Onesimus. Obviously Onesimus had disappointed his master, Philemon, and had been ineffectual. But he had repented, and Paul asked graciously if Philemon would receive Onesimus again. He requested that Onesimus be accepted not only as a servant, but also as a dear brother.

We don't read Philemon's answer, but according to Colossians 4:9, he responded in Christ's love and forgiveness. It speaks there of "Onesimus, a faithful and beloved brother, who is one of you." What a glorious picture of acceptance.

At times I am tempted to hold someone at arm's length because of a wrong he or she has done. But I have also hurt others. I want them to forgive me. Can I not also offer forgiveness and acceptance to others? If I do not forgive them, neither will God forgive me (Matthew 6:14-15).

It is good to hold up a high standard of holiness and purity, and to encourage those I love and know to walk in Christ. But may I never expect more of them than they are able to give.

It is, after all, only God in us who can do good. Any blessing I may be is because of Christ's life in mine. If I stop and consider Calvary's love, and realize all that Christ suffered for my sake, and how he daily offers forgiveness and cleansing, I will reach out to others in the same loving manner. Even if they do not meet my expectations.

prayer

Lord, I am sure that I disappoint you, but you forgive and heal my sins. Help me offer acceptance and forgiveness to others today.

reflection

Is someone failing to meet your expectations? How can you offer acceptance this week?

3

I'LL TAKE THE USUAL

2 Thessalonians 2:13-17

My dad and my uncles are set in their preferences and rarely change. My dad says, "If I like something, why would I change to something different? If I always choose the same dish, I know what I am getting, and I am always pleased." I like to try new recipes, but not for my dad and his brothers. They will not appreciate it at all.

They have schedules for their days, which vary only slightly. It is a dependable way to live. I was with them last week in their winter homes, and it brought order to life to know at what time something would happen each day. For example, at two o'clock we went for coffee, scarcely a minute early or late.

If we played shuffleboard, one uncle always took the black pucks, the other the yellow. Each had their certain chair and stick, and a certain one kept score. In culinary tastes, this standard is most pronounced: meat and potatoes, potatoes and meat. We laugh about their routines, but I realized this steadfastness carries over into their spiritual lives.

All three of these brothers are ministers. I love to hear them preach. Not because they hold up new philosophies, but because they preach Jesus. Over and over. It's Jesus, and him alone. Their preaching is no different from their lives. The only bright, new change they preach about is the hope of an immortal body and life in heaven.

The Bible speaks well of people who aren't quick to adopt every new idea and fashion, who hold steadfastly to the traditions of their fathers. Proverbs 22:28 says, "Remove not the ancient landmark."

In fulfilling the old law, Jesus did bring a new doctrine, that of a heart changed by his Spirit. The apostles of the early church were faithful in teaching this new gospel of Christ. We are blessed by having the New Testament, which clearly shows us a tradition of godly living portrayed by the disciples and the new churches, as recorded in the book of Acts.

Even if one's ancestors were not Christians, each of us has the tradition of the Bible to follow. After all, one's faith is personal. It doesn't hinge on whether my father or my grandfather were Christians; it depends on my own belief in Christ and my adherence to God's Word.

It doesn't matter how strictly my day is regimented, how consistently I follow a diet or daily planner. It's neither wrong nor right to eat meat and potatoes every day, and to have coffee at two in the afternoon.

It isn't wrong to adopt a new habit or to buy new things. But it is essential that I follow God's pattern for a holy life, and that I do not change in my loyalty to him.

prayer

Thank you, God, for giving me a legacy to follow—your Word that shows me the path of life. Keep me strong in your traditions of truth.

reflection

Are you a traditionalist? Or do you like to try new things? How can you be stable and yet embrace changing times?

4

LEFTOVERS OR RÉCHAUFFÉS?

Jeremiah 18:1-10

What do you do with the bits of food left over from dinner? Do you toss the leftovers, give it to the chickens, dish it into a small container for next day's lunch, push it to the back of the refrigerator and end up scrapping it the following week?

Or do you add a few more little bits of this and that and make a casserole? Some people turn up their noses at leftovers and refuse to eat anything they recognize from another meal. Others enjoy seeing how creative they can be with scraps of food. We were delighted to discover a new word for mundane leftovers: *réchauffés*, which simply means reheated food, but sounds like a fancy French dish. (In fact, the term does come from the French verb *réchauffers*, which means "to reheat.")

What may be trash to one is food for another. I like the challenge of making bits of leftovers into a new dish that still tastes fresh and new. Another name is "can't be duplicated." I have learned Mexican-style casseroles or burritos are easy to fix with a little rice, cheese, meat, and veggies from the leftover stash. Just add seasonings, a salad, salsa, and dressings, and presto—it's a new meal.

In our Scripture reading, God says that he is the true potter. The creator of human beings. He doesn't just throw us on the scrap pile when we don't meet his plan or fit into "his menu." But maybe he will turn us into something new and different.

As the Creator, God chose to make me just as I am. If I refuse to follow his plan, I have chosen to turn away as a discard. But if I am like moldable clay, or humble leftovers, he can make something useful of my life.

I think of people who have squandered many years living in sin. Does this mean they are only fit for scraps? Absolutely not. God can effectively use anyone who comes to him in repentance and humility. A friend of ours followed the world and Satan for years but, praise God, he repented. He grew very ill with cancer, but his wife, who had faithfully served God and raised a family alone, nursed him until his death. His testimony was incredible. "Once I was lost, but now I am found." Although he greatly regretted the wasted years, he was used for God's glory. It was in a different way than we had imagined, but his testimony was effective and blessed.

Sometimes I might think of myself as "leftovers"—no real good and too insignificant to be effective. But if I am willing to be used by God, and able to fit into a group of his people, I will find that my tiny effort, joined with the efforts of others, can form something new and "delicious," just as my casserole dish turns little bits of "nothings" into a tasty meal.

prayer

Lord, you have a plan for my life. Help me to follow your will. Show me how to bend to fit your pattern. And if you have to make something different than I wanted, help me to submit to that and still glorify your name.

reflection

Are you feeling like a leftover? Ask God to use you for his service today.

5

ONLY A CRUMB?

Mark 7:24-30

On Easter Sunday 2016, a Mennonite chorus sang at an evangelical church in San Salvador. As they sang, a man in the audience listened intently, tears streaming down his face. This is his story.

Over thirty years ago, when he was a young lad, this man attended a church in El Salvador where my friend's parents were missionaries. He was taken to church by a sweet elderly woman who loved God and wanted her neighbor children to hear about him. The little boy found Christ and salvation in that church. Two years later, the Mennonite church left that area, and he found another church to attend.

Now he pastors a Kentucky church and was back in San Salvador in March 2016 for a visit. It was the first time he'd seen Mennonites in thirty years. Small wonder he wept in remembrance of his childhood conversion and the ways his life was changed, first of all by his dear neighbor who walked with him to church, and then by hearing the Word of God preached in a way he understood.

Just a crumb? Maybe so, but it grew into a meal that has fed him for years. Does my faithfulness to God in little things matter? Absolutely.

I don't suppose the neighbor realized the impact she would have on this young man's life by introducing him to a Christian church. Likely she was also praying for him and may still not know how his life was changed by her influence.

The Mennonites at the earlier church didn't know what happened to the little boy. They had no idea that the seeds planted would grow and eventually nourish a church many miles away.

We may never know what our influence means to our neighbors, our friends, our family. It isn't important that we know. But it is important for us to keep faithful in all that God has called us to do, and to share the little crumbs of his truth to others.

Ecclesiastes 11:1 tells us to cast our bread upon the waters, and someday it will come back to us again. It doesn't say that we always will recognize the bread again, but perhaps you too can think of ways that God brought blessing into your life from someone you once helped.

Three years ago we visited some old friends. They used to live in my husband's community before we were married. The gentleman thanked my husband (again!) for the loan of a vehicle years ago when he was sent to hold meetings and his car had broken down. My husband couldn't remember the incident, but it was plain to see it was a crumb that had been a special memory to our friends all these years.

On the same trip we stayed with friends who showed hospitality and kindness. A crumb of blessing was presented when, just before we left, the host gathered his family around and together we prayed for safety on our journeys and for continued faithfulness to God.

I recall a verse written in a letter and a poem sent in a card. These were crumbs of blessing to encourage me and feed my soul.

prayer

Father, I am amazed at the ways you use our little crumbs. Bless the work of our hands and keep us faithful to tell others about your love.

reflection

Does it seem as if your crumbs are just crumbs? Thank God that you have crumbs to share, and ask him to multiply them for his purpose today.

6

BRING ON THE SALT

Colossians 4:1-6

I have tried cooking without salt, but the food was so bland that I gave it up. I know some people have to follow a salt-free diet for health. I suppose you could get used to it eventually, especially if your life depended on it, but it would be difficult. Salt just perks up a dish.

Many dishes need a mere hint of salt or seasoning to bring out their true flavor. An unusual spice might be just the thing to soften the tartness of a cranberry. Experimenting with seasonings adds zest to our meals.

My mother talks of a friend who tasted a cookie and said, "This has either a little too much allspice or not quite enough." We have chuckled about that over the years, but I wonder if my speech might be like that. Too spicy or not spicy enough?

In Matthew 5:13, Jesus calls his children the salt of the earth. Christians are to be holy, fine, and noble by God's grace and his goodness in their lives. Jesus asks what should be done if the salt isn't salty anymore, and then he answers his question—it must be thrown away because it is good for nothing.

I trust the influence in the communities where Christians live is not salt gone bad but rather a seasoning of God's grace. Salt preserves. May I preserve the truth of God's Word and also preserve faith in my heart.

Too much salt is not good. My sister pours salt on popcorn to the point that my dad says that it grinds between the teeth. Can my speech be too salty? God requires moderation in everything we do, so yes, even in my salt.

Salt creates thirst. Especially after a crunch or two of that popcorn, we're hunting for a glass of water. Can my life make others thirst for more of God? Oh, may it be so. May my speech honor God; may my dress, behavior, driving habits, and simple courtesy at the checkout show others God lives within me. May these gentle actions bring just enough salt into their lives that they too will seek to drink from the water of life.

I am blessed by friends and sisters whose attitudes of reverence to God challenge me. They turn our conversations to God, and sometimes I go home and search out a Scripture verse they quoted. In that way they are being salty.

We have been taught by practice and by preaching to conduct regular times of family worship. It's an excellent time to explain songs and Bible passages. I pray God will use this time to create a thirst for Christ in our children's hearts.

"Have salt in yourselves, and have peace with another" (Mark 9:50). Truly if I am salty in thirsting for God and salty in preserving faith and in adding God's savor to my lives, I will live peacefully with others.

Add salt to your spiritual diet, and you won't be the only one who benefits.

prayer

Lord, make me salty and also thirsty for you. Let my salt never lose its flavor but find its saltiness by meditating on your Word.

reflection

Do you feel bland? How can you salt your life and your words so others too are thirsty for God?

7

BREAKING OF BREAD

Mark 8:1-21

Eating together often shows a comradeship and opens my heart to share more than bread. The Bible mentions many times that people ate together. In Acts 2:42 and 46 it is called "breaking of bread."

Luke, in chapter 24, relates an experience two friends had as they trudged the long, dusty road to Emmaus. Disheartened, they left Jerusalem after Jesus' cruel trial and death. God brought hope in the very form and presence of Jesus. He joined them and asked why they were so dejected, then explained complex Scriptures they didn't understand. They didn't recognize him until they reached their home and Jesus blessed and broke the bread. Later, as they shared the story with others, they remembered their hearts began burning as Jesus walked and talked with them.

I might have an Emmaus road to travel—a long and lonely pathway with turnings I don't understand. Jesus may not come as a physical person, but he is here. When I open my heart to his word and let him break the bread of life to me, my heart burns with love for him and acceptance of the road.

I sense Jesus also understands the importance of the natural breaking of bread. When I was a child it was expected for my family to be at home at mealtimes. Even though some had school to attend and others had day jobs, we usually ate breakfast and supper together. It formed a closeness and kept relationships current.

This has become a routine since my marriage too, and one I appreciate. As schedules become full—with eight people coming and going this is often true—we have to make family mealtime a conscious effort.

It is essential to keep the atmosphere around the table calm and free of stress. It's hard to digest food when my stomach is in knots because of a disagreement. Although trouble is part of life, the simple act of sitting together with my family brings a measure of peace. This is a time when we share the happenings of the day and ask advice for a complexity.

I save tidbits to share from conversations or letters I know will interest my family. We laugh and learn together. It's not unusual to pull out a dictionary or an atlas to settle a discussion. We help each other with table manners and encourage each other with ideas and inspirations.

I can imagine Jesus and his disciples eating fish fried on the shore (John 21:13) and mealtime at Martha's table (John 12). I think Jesus enjoyed this time of breaking bread with those he loved. It was in these times that he taught them where to go for the bread of life. He was that bread, and how he longed for them to understand.

If he fills and feeds me, I am truly satisfied. The world offers to feed me with exciting books, movies, clothes, and music. But these will only leave my soul even hungrier and emptier. God alone feeds the soul. When I have eaten from his Word and find my soul growing strong and healthy, I can reach out to others and share with them this wonderful life-saving Bread.

God has promised that someday we may gather around an eternal table. "Let us be glad and rejoice, and give honour to him: for the marriage of the Lamb is come and his wife [those have their sins washed away in Jesus' blood] hath made herself ready" (Revelation 19:7). The heavenly breaking of bread is beyond my imaginations, and I long for that day.

prayer

Father of life, and bread of heaven, I long to be fed from your Word so that the hunger of my soul is filled. Help me to daily eat from your table and to share your goodness with others.

reflection

Are you breaking bread with Jesus? Do you have spiritual bread to share with others?

1

GLORIOUS WITHIN

1 Peter 3:1-12

She is beautiful," someone said. I thought, really? No, she is not very attractive in facial feature and form. But she is beautiful. Why? Her spirit is alive with God's peace, her eyes radiate his joy, her hands reach out with his love.

"She too is beautiful," another said. She was? Her hair was missing after chemotherapy, gray skin stretched over sharp bones, cheeks were sunken. But she was beautiful. Why? She knew the Lord and loved him with all her heart. Even as death cast its shadow over her body, her spirit lived victoriously, aglow with a heavenly light.

One of my church sisters is beautiful by the dedication she shows in caring for her family. Living with a son who is autistic brings challenges to each day. Yet she never complains, only lovingly, graciously serves him with Christ's love. Her attitude of acceptance and gratitude inspires me.

These ladies discovered the secret of true beauty.

Years ago a friend penned Psalm 45:13 in my autograph book (remember those little booklets we passed around, collecting poems, verses, and autographs?): "The king's daughter is all glorious within." It was the first time I heard that verse, and it has often encouraged me to cultivate God's graces in my soul, mind, and heart and to put less emphasis on my appearance.

That doesn't mean I may be lazy in dress and manner and shun exercise, good eating habits, and cleanliness. God requires orderly conduct (1 Corinthians 14:40); the fear, or reverence, of the Lord is clean (Psalm 19:9). My body is the temple of God (1 Corinthians

6:19) and, as such, I should care for it wisely and keep it holy and pure for him.

I can be clean and neat without placing undue emphasis on my looks. A regular bath and hair-washing routine makes anyone attractive. I want Christ to be seen in a body that is worthy of him.

But if I spend too much time worrying about looking pretty and too much money on all the latest products that promise smooth skin and silky hair, I will find myself distracted from following after God and his righteousness. Life is not about me. It's about my Lord.

No matter how my features are arranged, I can be beautiful when my life is patterned after his will and I am filled with his grace and virtue. May I hear "She is beautiful" from God's viewpoint.

prayer

Lord, you are the giver of life and health. I am created in your image and have your life within and that makes me beautiful. Help me to cultivate your graces day by day.

reflection

Do you struggle with feeling unlovely? Cultivate the beauty of Jesus and embrace your body, as it is in his image and is his dwelling place.

2

GOD'S HEALTH PLAN

Psalm 103

*D*oes God have a health plan? I love the picture I get from
John's words in 3 John 2: "Beloved, I wish above all things
that thou mayest prosper and be in health, even as thy soul pros-
pereth." Most important is having a soul that is alive and growing
toward God. If my health matches that, God be praised.

Health is important to God. He says in Exodus 15:26, "I am the
Lord that healeth thee." Today's reading lists some of God's blessings upon us; in verse 3, forgiveness of sins comes before "healeth all
thy diseases." God can heal and often does. Sometimes he heals by
giving the sick one eternal life in heaven rather than physical health.

Not all are created equally, and some struggle all their lives with
sickness. Others reach a grand old age with no major problems.
Some may have frequent hospital stays, while others seldom see a
doctor. Some follow strict regimens of diet and vitamins and still
battle illness, while others eat what they wish and still keep fit.

I can never begin to understand why life is like that and why a
perfect God allows sickness, pain, and death. But I know he is God
and he is good. Since the fall of man in the garden of Eden in Genesis 3 and when God gave us the ability to choose, evil things are a
part of life.

A few years ago my aunt learned she had diabetes. She faithfully followed a diabetic diet and kept fit by working in gardens and
flower beds. Last week she was diagnosed with cancer. Does it make
sense? Not to any of us. I long, as John in the Bible longed for Gaius,
for my aunt's health to prosper as her soul does. Her husband, my
uncle, was also bursting with vigor until a lung disease took his life

five years ago. It doesn't seem fair for their family to be facing this affliction. But we trust God. He knows, he cares, he loves.

I wish we could buy health. Somehow we would scrape up the money and purchase a long, sound life. But it isn't possible. My life and the lives of those I love are in the hands of God. He has promised that heaven will not have any health concerns or terminal illnesses. "In the midst of [heaven] . . . was there the tree of life . . . and the leaves of the tree were for the healing of the nations" (Revelation 22:2).

Oh, what a glorious day that will be—when we will all be whole and healthy, with strong bodies and sound minds that won't decay or deteriorate. I will sign up for God's eternal health plan!

prayer

God and creator of life and health, I thank you for giving me breath and strength. I pray for those in poor health. May each of us have a soul that is prospering for you.

reflection

Are you often sick? How can you find peace in subscribing to God's health plan? If you know others who are ill, how can you reach out to them in an ongoing way?

3

BEAUTY CARE
FOR THE EYES

2 Corinthians 10

Eyes tell a story. They show excitement, anticipation, worry, fear, a troubled conscience, or fatigue and ill health. Eyes sparkle with vigor or are peacefully restful. Eyes express torment or hate. Eyes are rightly called the window of the soul.

My nephew's eyes often mirror mischief that lurks in his young mind. You just never know what he's up to. He can't hide his feelings, and if he has a great idea—look out. He might be digging for worms even when no one is going fishing or clipping his toenails until they bleed. He could be scratching his name on the lampstand or drawing with a crayon on the baseboard. Watch those eyes!

More than just the health of my eyes, what I am looking at is important. My sister-in-Christ always looks for the good in others. She is cheerful even when tired and forgiving even when someone has been unkind. If I need health tips, she drops what she's doing and comes to my rescue. She spends hours serving her widowed father-in-law, who lives next door. Her eyes and her life are beautiful.

Today's Scripture lists many ideas to make my vision beautiful. I can look beyond the outward appearance. Anyone may wear a mask, and being well-dressed or wealthy is not a criterion for spiritual beauty.

Comparing my looks, my weight, my shoe size, and my circumstances with anyone else's is sure to bring discontentment and perhaps even envy and anger. The apostle Paul states it simply: to do so is foolish.

God made me as I am. I can always try to improve my life by diet and exercise, by reading godly books, by befriending godly people. But first of all I must accept myself as God made me. He is the creator and his plan is perfect. If I am constantly chafing against my appearance, wishing I were different, I am like the person spoken about in Romans 9:20: "O man, who art thou that repliest against God? Shall the thing formed say to him that formed it, Why hast thou made me thus?"

Beautiful eyes view God as sovereign and just and see, in return, a person with abilities and attributes he saw fit to give. Beautiful eyes look for the good and true in others. A sister-in-Christ is a challenge to me in this. She inspires me by freely expressing gratitude, by focusing on what others do well, and by reminding me that my attitude toward life is more important than the circumstances themselves. She looks for ways to be a witness to her neighbors, her grandchildren, and the children she befriended while she worked at a school cafeteria. Her eyes are beautiful.

"O our God . . . our eyes are upon thee" (2 Chronicles 20:12). Keeping my eyes fixed on Jesus will keep them from wandering to worldly temptations or from pinpointing the faults of others.

Beautiful eyes are pure. They sparkle with God's joy because he is my life.

prayer

Lord, I long to have beautiful eyes. Fill my heart with your peace so I can view you as God and myself as your servant. Keep my eyes from looking enviously at others or being tempted by sin.

reflection

What are your eyes seeing today? Is your gaze pointed heavenward?

4

BEAUTIFUL LIPS

James 3

A few friends stand out who have beautiful lips because they speak gracious words. One sister in church kindly clasped my hand and sweetly said a few words of encouragement on a day I was feeling sad. Another wished God's blessings on a new venture. Every time I speak with still another friend, I am inspired because she always leaves me with something that reminds me of God.

On the day I wrecked our car, I trembled the whole way home. When I reached school to pick up the children, a church sister came over and said, tears in her eyes and love in her voice, "Faith, I prayed for you all morning!" I know others were praying too, but to this day my heart is still warmed by the verbalizing of her thoughtfulness.

A word of appreciation for a job well done or even for a willing effort builds confidence to keep on trying. A word of comfort when others are grieving helps them to know I care. It may be just a word, but it can brighten someone's day—or crush her heart. May I share only beautiful words.

The famous Proverbs 31 woman is known for her wise speech and kind words. "In her tongue is the law of kindness" (verse 26). I ponder that. The law of kindness. Doesn't that imply a rule of life? If my life is governed by gentleness, my speech will be kind.

Today's Scripture passage assures me that what is in my heart comes out of my mouth. I can't hide my feelings for long; they will slip out in a hasty word or explanation. The secret is to guard my thoughts well, and then my lips will speak graciously.

Sometimes I have to stop myself and ask, "Why do I feel this way? Why am I biting back a nasty retort?" Usually it stems from a wrong attitude I must root out and destroy. By claiming God's power and the blood of Christ, I can be free from unloving thoughts.

Conversation is a part of life, an interesting part. Words convey so much, and I learn to know people by talking with them. I can use words to explain, encourage, bless, edify, and serve. Or I can use them to wound, destroy a reputation, gossip, and complain.

My lips are most beautiful when they are praising God. "My lips shall greatly rejoice when I sing unto thee. . . . My tongue also shall talk of thy righteousness all the day long" (Psalm 71:23-24). Sharing the testimony of what God has done and is doing for me is a way to develop beautiful lips. And, of course, anyone can smile. You never know what a heartfelt smile will do for another person.

If I am filled with God's wisdom, he can teach me when to speak and what to say. Sometimes I have to speak painful words to help someone. Proverbs 27:6 says, "Faithful are the wounds of a friend," and the apostle Paul writes about "speaking the truth in love" (Ephesians 4:15). Even when I must share a word of concern, I can do it with love and grace. God can show me how. By his grace, my lips can be beautiful for him.

prayer

Father, I long to have beautiful lips, to speak words of grace. Keep my heart filled with your wisdom and direct my speech.

reflection

Does someone need an encouraging word? Speak it!

5

BEAUTIFUL HANDS

Matthew 8:1-17

*Y*esterday the church trustees hosted a "work bee" to clear a space for a school ball field. Everyone was busy. Trees were cut, pulled to an open area, sawed into logs, split, and stacked into pickup beds. Wood was quickly delivered—"Who needs firewood? Here's a pile!"—and the truck was reloaded. Small lads kept water pitchers filled and cups passed. A few ladies provided a tasty meal to feed us. It was a wonderful picture of working together with our hands to bless others. The firewood will warm many families next winter, and the cleared field will be a delightful spot for the schoolchildren.

My aunt sends many cards; another friend has sewn hundreds of quilts for relief efforts. Our little sewing circle stitches blankets for the poor. And day by day, I see opportunities to bless others. It might be making a phone call, sending a letter, or taking a basket of fruit. Let my hands be beautiful for Christ!

Recently our minister's father died. His three married children and their families immediately prepared for a lengthy trip. Some sisters went to help with work at their homes, others fixed snacks and activities for the long drive, some sewed clothes, and others babysat while the mothers packed. Somehow they all got ready, and later when one expressed her thanks, I thought of how this was what God calls us to: service to others.

Jesus is our blessed example. We have record of only three years of his ministry, but during that time his hands were busy. Healing, serving, blessing, leading. At the end of that time, his loving hands were cruelly hammered onto a tree, and there he gave the last greatest gift—salvation!

Can my hands be like Jesus' hands? I look at my hands—they certainly are not beautiful. Long, wide fingers, knobby knuckles, scars, crooked joints, and bulging veins aren't on anyone's list of beautiful features. But the work of my hands may be beautiful if it is done for others in Christ's name. It doesn't need to be a great and wondrous work either. Jesus says that even a cup of cold water shared in his name is blessed by God.

prayer

Lord, your requirements for beautiful hands are a loving heart and a servant attitude. Help me to mirror you today and reach out in love to bless others.

reflection

What "cup of cold water" can you give to someone today?

6

BEAUTIFUL FEET

Isaiah 52:7-10

I never paid much attention to my feet until they started ach-
ing. I ran through most of my life barefooted. Now I find it
pays to wear shoes with good support. A simple thing, but still
an adjustment.

When I'm looking for beauty I usually skip the feet, but the
Bible speaks in several places of beautiful feet. How can my feet be
beautiful? God's beauty standards differ from the world's. He does
not mean beautiful to look at—he asks my feet to run to serve others
and to spread the message of his love.

In the list of the Christian's armor in Ephesians 6, it gives the
requirement for my footwear: "Feet shod with the preparation of
the gospel of peace" (verse 15). Feet that come in peace and love are
truly beautiful feet. They are also feet ready to stand strong in the
battle I daily face against the devil.

Proverbs 6 lists seven things God hates. Among them, "feet that
be swift in running to mischief." I hate to think my feet could be
ugly to God, but they are if they run to be first to share a morsel of
gossip, to harshly scold someone, or to cook up cruel tricks to play
on someone.

Last night my feet were weary from hard work. Sometimes my
spirit sags too. I love the promise in Isaiah 40: "They that wait upon
the Lord shall renew their strength; they shall mount up with wings
as eagles; they shall run, and not be weary; and they shall walk, and
not faint" (verse 31).

My cousin briskly climbed mountains and hiked paths last
week, inspiring my admiration. More than that accomplishment, I

appreciate her willingness to help an overbearing neighbor who kept calling at all hours, forgetting that my cousin's travels took her to a time zone three hours away. I also admire her kind patience with her elderly parents. Her feet are beautiful because they serve others.

A sister-in-Christ serves by taking a weekly meal to our widowed pastor. I'm sure some weeks she gets weary of it, as her family also operates a bakery. Her husband is one of our ministers and a busy man. But she never frets that it makes her Tuesdays too full. She just faithfully keeps cooking.

Beautiful feet walk in the paths of Jesus, following his call. They serve him by ministering to needs around them. They show love by taking his message of salvation to sin-stained souls. In his grace, my feet can be beautiful.

prayer

Lord, make my feet beautiful for you! I long to walk sturdily and faithfully in your ways, sharing your message of peace.

reflection

Do your feet often ache? How can you develop beautiful feet, starting today?

7

POISE AND GRACE

Hebrews 12:1-14

Some people are naturally graceful. They walk with elegance and confidence. Others shuffle along, with drooping shoulders and awkward steps. It doesn't seem to matter how slim or how heavy one is. Some large people walk gracefully while the tiny-framed ones are hunched over.

I don't think God cares about the manner in which I walk, but that my inner soul is strong in his grace. How can I walk with confidence? By recognizing his claim on my life, by walking close to him in daily Bible reading and prayer, by trusting him to guide me through dark spots and across bumpy paths.

How can I make a straight path, as our Scripture reading for today instructs?

I think of my sister, who offers to take another's turn driving children to school when she knows someone's schedule is especially full. She has been known to clean the church house when it's not her turn, to lighten another's load. She drops off homemade grape nuts to the families who thoroughly enjoy them but cannot make the time-consuming cereal. It's not that my sister has so little to do—but she orders her life by God's grace and so blesses others.

In many little ways I also can walk in God's grace, even when my natural gait isn't particularly graceful. I know he is beside me, helping me over the mountains or around the shadowy corners, and that gives me assurance to walk boldly.

One of my dear friends has been a faithful member of the Mennonite church for many years, while her husband chooses not to attend with her. I wonder how my friend keeps on when so much of our lives revolve around church activities. But she practices submissive love and is committed to respecting and honoring her husband. She doesn't attend weeknight services if he requests that and she refuses to argue about differing views on Scripture. Her Christian poise challenges my own commitment.

God hasn't promised an easy life, one that glides downhill. But he has promised to walk with us each step of the way. Because I claim that promise, I walk confidently and joyfully.

prayer

Dear Lord and Master, thank you for the promise that I need never walk alone. I claim your grace to walk in courage through each day and over each rocky path.

reflection

Are you trudging along, weary and defeated? Today, claim God's promises, clasp his hand, lift your head, and walk boldly!

1

ONE MORE BRICK

Psalm 18:33-39, 46, 49

*M*y friend struggles to nourish her little ones. It is difficult to find food that agrees with them and nurtures growth. She also battles health issues and finds it a challenge to be strong emotionally. Added to that is the care of aging parents. At times the demands of life overwhelm her. Some days she feels confident she will be able to cope—and even to accomplish her goals for the week. Then someone will ask her to drop what she's doing to help them. It can create resentment even while she longs to love. Often she cries for God's grace to keep walking, keep holding on, keep loving.

"It's all those bricks," someone told her. Bricks? Yes, bricks. We each have an allotment for the day. If we're given an extra brick to carry, we have to drop one of the previously collected bricks. For example, today I might plan to do laundry, bake cookies, and write a letter. If someone asks me to take an elderly friend to town, I have to eliminate one or more of my planned tasks. If tomorrow looks equally busy, I can become resentful.

I admire my friend's response: "As unto Jesus." That's how she serves the ones she loves. Yes, she does love them, even when they make requests that infringe upon her time, health, and spirits. She brings joy to her parents by her daily care, and she often takes time to listen to those who are hurting. She has known deep sorrow, and through trusting in the Savior, her soul has become polished like a diamond God has refined.

Days are not always easy, and I am not always courageous. Some days the bricks feel too heavy for me. They seem to be dropping around me, and maybe they'll smash my toes. I cringe as I look for a way to hide. Then I open the trusty Word of God. I have learned that no matter the size or number of bricks, God's words bring courage to my heart.

I realize again he is the source of all I need. I can keep walking in his strength when my own is spent. He will not require more of me than I can do or give. Most of all, he promises to keep my soul strong in his grace. He helps me surrender my plans to his will; then, when they are rearranged, I can exchange one brick for another without resentment.

prayer

Lord, some days I am so weary of facing the heavy bricks. Teach me to find strength and courage from you, in seeking your words of promise. Thank you for carrying me through this day.

reflection

Do you resent a change of plans? How can you carry your bricks with joy?

2

MY DAY IS TOO SHORT

Psalm 119:9-16, 97-104

As long as I remember, we've been taught that daily Bible study is of highest importance to a Christian. I love the time alone with God and his Word. My soul is nurtured, blessed, strengthened, and convicted.

But what if the day's too short to find that alone time? One summer I felt overwhelmed by life's demands. Our fourth baby was fussy, and I spent hours comforting and rocking. It was gardening time, and you can't put beans on hold while you care for the baby. It was also the summer our church decided it was time to remodel the church house. My husband was elected for the building committee, so he was usually gone four nights a week and Saturdays.

Each day seemed like a struggle for survival. I was often exhausted because the baby was up at night, and with four little ones (the oldest not quite seven) it was hard to get much of a nap during the day. I tried to hurriedly read a chapter from the Bible as I fed the baby, but it was so rushed. I felt guilty, even condemned, because I was missing my morning hour with God.

Then God spoke to me. One night as I fed the baby, I cried out, tears of frustration washing my face. God seemed to say, "It's okay. I know you love me. Think of the verses you memorized. Meditate on those. They will feed your soul until your life is quieter."

I gasped and stopped rocking. Yes! I had memorized many chapters and verses over the years. Quietly I recited one chapter and meditated on its words of truth. In peace I went back to bed; in serenity

I arose in the morning. Throughout the next day the verses spoke to my heart, and I cherished the feeling of closeness to my Lord.

The next night I recited a different set of verses and was again blessed by the presence of God. The guilt was gone—erased by God's enduring love and replaced by his strengthening joy.

Those hectic days passed, as all days do, but the memory of that time still brings comfort. No matter what my need, God provides soul and spirit food. Sometimes it might be through a verse I scribble on my weekly planner. It is a blessing to keep scripture verses penned and placed by the kitchen or laundry sink to study as we work. We have taped verses to the dashboard of the car to read or review when traffic is stopped.

While a time of daily meditation is ideal and something to strive for, God understands if a day passes when I simply did not have that hour. As long as my heart is longing for him and I seek him daily in prayer, he will show me how to find time for my soul to be replenished, even if it's in the middle of the night.

prayer

Father God, thank you for showing me your love and your grace. Thank you for being there for me when I found it hard to be there with you.

reflection

Do you struggle to find time alone with God? Pray earnestly for him to show you a way to daily be nourished in the Word. He will provide!

3

MOVING STRESS

Mark 6:30-46

Maybe you're one who has lived in the same house all your life, or in the same community, or even in the same state. If so, this stress is foreign to you. I was born in Virginia, but my family moved to Pennsylvania when I was one, to Missouri when I was ten, and then to another location in Missouri when I was nineteen. During my marriage we have moved four times, and the last move relocated us by eighteen hundred miles.

Moving carries unique stresses. There are decisions by the dozens—and that's before you pack the first box. To save or sell? To pack or pitch? To paint the house or just clean it? To sell by a realtor or personally?

Before we moved to Missouri we also had end-of-year school activities to squeeze in. Field trips, program, picnic, and teacher gifts, as well as farewell tokens for our friends. We also visited our relatives in Ohio, arranged bank changes, and gathered dental and medical records.

I can't imagine my mother had even one minute to spare, but one special day is riveted in my mind. My dad took the day off and we dropped the sorting and packing. We packed a picnic lunch and headed to a lake. There we rented boats and spent a relaxing day as a family. Possibly some jobs never got done, but does it matter now?

I always knew my parents loved us, but that day I was convinced that no one had a family as special as ours. It wasn't an expensive cruise, but to a little girl it was invaluable.

It's not that we weren't busy. We lived on a dairy farm, my father worked in construction, and later we operated a bakery for four years. But our parents often took us to the zoo, we played games as a family, we read together. Simple things, but they refreshed our spirits to face the rigors of the day.

Jesus told his disciples to take time off to renew their souls. They had been bombarded by people seeking miracles and those hungry to hear Christ's words. The disciples didn't have time even to eat. I am rarely that busy, but I still fill our days with more than enough to do, especially when I'm moving. Jesus did the tasks that needed to be done, then he rested. It's an example for me. No matter how hectic my schedule or how many decisions I face, if I take time to refresh my spirit, the jobs get done more quickly and the decisions are made more easily.

The last part of Ezekiel 11:16 has taken on new meaning for me during especially busy times: "Yet will I be to them as a little sanctuary in the countries where they shall come." God is my safe place, my sanctuary. May I always run to him when I feel overwhelmed.

prayer

Lord, you understood the value of time to rest and renew your soul. Keep my heart focused on you and help me to realize when I also need to take time apart and rest.

reflection

Are you in the middle of a move? Or just having a hectic time of work? Plan a day, an hour, to rest and refresh yourself.

4

PEER PRESSURE

1 Corinthians 3

Carefully I scanned my children. Did they look neat enough? Cute enough? Were their clothes modern and in style? Shouldn't I stop in town and buy sweaters and shoes that weren't so old-fashioned? The ones they were wearing were out-of-date hand-me-downs.

I told my husband about my misgivings and he wisely counseled me, "Are you dressing them to make a statement or to please God? Does it matter what others think, if the children are modest and clean? Why do you care?"

I cringed when I discovered I cared because of pride and peer pressure. Both hit me at once; they threatened my peace, not to mention my wallet. But surrendered to God, pride and pressure had to back off. Buying unnecessary clothes just to look modern isn't wise.

Another pressure I face is trying to do too much so no one thinks I'm a slacker. Do you need cookies for a school function? I can bake them. Would someone type a new cleaning chart? Consider it done. You need a ride to the airport? Just what I wanted to do. And on and on. I can't be seen as inadequate to any task. I've got this!

But God isn't looking for someone to do it all. He wants, most of all, a heart that seeks to serve and praise him first and always. If I am focused on being busy and on top of things, I won't have time I need to cultivate a restful heart.

Peer pressure pokes its aggravating nose into the dishes I fix for a fellowship meal at church. It wants me to prepare the best and most expensive menus and decorate accordingly. That pressure can influence me to dress in uncomfortable shoes just to look smart.

I am thankful God has answers to this problem, just as he has for everything I face. Our daily Bible reading reminds me that I can plant, that someone else might water, but God is the only one who can bring an increase. He also shows me that we work together as Christians, and it's not me alone against the world.

My work will be tested. If it's built upon pride and peer pressure, it's guaranteed to burn, as dry straw does, in the spiritual fire of God's refining. But if I build all my labor upon the one Foundation, Jesus Christ, it will stand the test.

Does it matter how my family and I look, dress, cook, manage, and work? Of course it matters. But the bottom line is that "we are Christ's." Working for any other reason than to honor him is a vain pursuit. Learning to accept my limitations, even when I have to say no to requests, brings peace.

prayer

Jesus, I come to you, seeking to honor you alone. Thank you for being the Rock on which I can build my life. Help all my decisions to be guided by your will.

reflection

Do you feel pressured to buy or do things to please others? How can you seek to order your days in a way that pleases God?

5

STORMS OF ADVERSITY

2 Corinthians 4

One of my friends has faced hardships over and over. Her mother has multiple sclerosis, and growing up my friend had to take charge of the home at a young age. Additional health issues afflict the family. Her mother has had numerous surgeries and needs nearly full-time care. Her brother-in-law died of cancer. A young niece is taking cancer treatments. Her marriage faced traumas most of ours have not. Many days are full of pain, stress, adversity, and grief.

Is there any encouragement I can give? My life seems lily-pad balmy in comparison, and many of my adversities have been spiritual, emotional, and relational. Do I ask God for suffering so I have words of grace to share with her?

Pointing her and all those who are facing difficulties to the One who does know and love and care is something basic I can do. Jesus' life was not easy, and he endured extreme pain and desperation, even death, in a human body.

Finding courage to be faithful in the middle of the storm of adversity is a challenge all of us face. Have I understood how the apostle Paul could say he was troubled but not distressed, perplexed but not in despair, persecuted but not forsaken, cast down but not destroyed?

Perhaps part of the answer lies in verse 7 of our passage today. The treasure we have is God's Spirit within; and yes, it is kept in an earthen vessel: a body that hurts, suffers, and dies. Because of this humanness we cling to the God who is eternal, so that we acknowledge him as our Power and not our own pitiful ability.

My grandma showed the truth of verses 15 and 16, which I paraphrase: "Because of God's abundant grace, in thanksgiving for his glory, we don't faint or falter in trials. Even though our outward body is deteriorating, our souls are growing stronger every day." Why? Because Grandma didn't focus on the pain of today but rather on the glory which would come. Though she is now deceased, we trust she is experiencing that release from pain and suffering.

I love the testimony of a brother whose family stood firm through the crises of several church divisions. When I asked his wife how they could still be true to the church without becoming bitter, she humbly replied, "We chose to focus on God and not on people. People will fail. God is faithful, and because of him we can be faithful as well."

The things we see are here and now. But the things we live for are "there and then" for eternity. God, grant that our hearts will cling to you no matter how fierce the storms of adversity pound. Remember, the Lord walked through the storm and he is still walking through it with us.

prayer

God, remind me that storms are only in this life. Heaven will truly be worth the struggle for life, trust, and faith. Keep my eyes focused on you alone.

reflection

Does life seem too hard to bear? Sit at the feet of the One who bore all suffering for you, and feel his compassion and his strength.

6

INTERRUPTIONS
AND IRRITATIONS

Psalm 46

She can cut and sew a dress in three hours," I sighed, watching our schoolteacher's machine whizzing along. Her mother looked at me sympathetically and said, "Remember, you have interruptions."

Ah, yes, interruptions. Children. "Mama, can you help me?" "Mama, come and see." "Mama, I need a drink." "Mama, he hit me."

It's not just mothers who face interruptions. Everyone does to one extent or another. Teachers have students who need aid; nurses have patients who exact patience; store clerks have customers looking for items; retirees have calls, letters, or emails to answer and people to visit.

People drop by unannounced. How do I respond? Do they sense frustration from me or a welcoming spirit?

And the irritations. They can be as intense as a flat tire when you're on a tight schedule or as mild as a lost mitten. Just now we're facing one: a lost suitcase. A trip to Montana was therefore challenged by the loss of clothes and of gifts I had made. It was easy to feel frustrated and out of control.

My sister reminded me to give it to God. The suitcase? Of course. I am quick to say all I have is God's, so it surely includes lost luggage. He knows where it is and whether I have more lessons to learn through this irritation.

In our Bible reading, the psalmist tells me to be still and know that God is God. He is Lord of my schedule, if I allow him to be. His peace is a promise when I surrender my struggles to him. John 14 is a chapter that encourages me as I study the gentle words of Jesus. "Let not your heart be troubled. . . . Peace I leave with you. . . . He that hath my commandments, and keepeth them, he it is that loveth me: and he that loveth me shall be loved of my Father."

So how do I face the interruptions and irritations that will most certainly come? It is important for my heart to be calm. Even when I feel like flying off the handle, if I stop to whisper a prayer, God can bring serenity to my flustered mind. His Spirit can help mine respond properly without anger and frustration.

Once a friend and her mother stopped in for an hour. I was in the middle of a messy painting project, but on that day, this was an interruption that inspired and blessed me. After they left I was so invigorated that I finished the painting in record time. I thanked God for sending these friends my way.

It reminded me that if I surrender my schedule, even the interruptions can be part of God's plan.

prayer

Lord, I wonder what irritation or interruption I will face today. Help me to meet each one with your grace.

reflection

Are you frustrated by a change of plans? How can you know Jesus' promised peace in the middle of the upheaval?

7

SUFFERING

1 Peter 4

*N*early every winter, pneumonia ravaged my father's health. His first introduction to the dreaded disease was double pneumonia at twelve days old. When he was in his sixties, he failed a stress test, so he was admitted to the hospital for a heart procedure. After the surgery, the pulmonary specialist discovered a disease turning his lungs to leather. It was much more serious than the heart problem. With regular medication, Dad finally made it through winters without contracting pneumonia.

I remember the fear I faced during his heart surgery, and the relief when it was over. Only to realize it wasn't over. The lung specialist scared us with his concern, and Dad was hospitalized for days. But God took a hard thing and turned it into something good—a remedy for his lung condition.

Suffering is never pleasant. Today's reading speaks of different kinds of suffering. If I suffer consequences because I have done wrong, it's no more than I deserve. But if I suffer because of Christ, I am part of him and his sufferings.

We are part of the body of Christ and members of each other. First Corinthians 12 reminds us that if one member suffers, the other members also suffer. For example, if I pinch my finger in a door, my other hand comforts it; my feet run for aid, my voice cries for help, blood cells rush to the point of impact to aid the healing process. Likewise, when I hear of Christians in other countries suffering for their faith, it should hurt me too.

God can use their suffering to help me become more compassionate and less selfish.

Seeing the sufferings of those who are often in physical pain can teach me to reach out in love to alleviate their afflictions in some way. I have seen beautiful souls emerge from suffering. In that way God is bringing good out of bad things that we would never choose or wish on anyone.

If I accept pain as a part of this fallen world and refuse to allow any bitter thought to rise against God, he can use suffering to create something beautiful in my life.

When I knew someone I loved was dying, I had the opportunity to say "I love you." It was also a reminder to say those loving words to the people in my life who are strong and healthy, as I realized those could be the last words they hear from me.

Sufferings can bring my soul closer to God. One friend lost her husband in an accident only a few days after their wedding. She said, "I know better than ever that God is all I need." Another widow has the testimony of feeling overwhelmed by God's presence: "I never felt this close to him when my husband was alive. But God is my all in all."

Can suffering bring good? Yes, if I allow God to do his gracious work of redemption in my heart.

prayer

Father God, I don't understand why those I love suffer. I only know that you can bring something good from the worst thing I can imagine, just as the death of your dear Son brought life to eternal souls. For that I thank you.

reflection

Are you or someone you love suffering? Can you find blessings that are arising because of this suffering?

1

THE ULTIMATE
SACRIFICE

Hebrews 7:25-28; 9:6-15, 24-28

acrifice signifies giving up, a surrender. In the Old Testament, sacrifices were literal: beasts were offered to God on altars of stone.

I dislike dealing with the blood and meat of a dead animal. As a farming family, we raised cows, hogs, and chickens for our consumption. On butchering days I tried to find a job cooking for the workers or babysitting. Anything was preferred to handling dead animals.

So when I read through the book of Leviticus, I wonder how a squeamish stomach would have survived in the days of continual sacrifices. According to Levitical law, God required offerings for every imaginable sin. Included in the list is the offense of being with an unclean person. Uncleanness came from contact with sick or disabled people or animals, or a dead or injured body. It would have taken amazing skill to remember the law in its entirety.

Although the priests regularly offered sacrifices for the people, once a year they had a solemn ceremony. The high priest made his ritual washing, then entered the holy of holies, a sacred place reserved for him alone to meet with God. There he offered a special sacrifice for all the offenses the people had committed throughout the year and had perhaps forgotten or missed in their confessions.

Think of carrying guilt for a year—and then imagine the incredible relief pardon brought! Their sins were obliterated—completely washed away . . . but only for that moment. They were human, just as we are, and without the indwelling presence of the Holy

Spirit, their sins soon started piling up again, waiting for the next yearly sacrifice.

Everything God does has a purpose. The Old Testament is full of shadows that are symbols of a new and better way. In 1 Chronicles 17, it tells of God redeeming the people; Isaiah 19:20 says God will send a Savior to redeem them. This redemption was perfect, not a mere ritual that lasted briefly, but one that brought a complete change of heart and life.

Jesus is the spotless Lamb, the ultimate sacrifice. Because of his sacrifice at Calvary, we no longer need to offer animals on a literal altar. The first time I realized what my salvation cost, I wept. Here was blood and atonement. Here was the offering to end all offerings. Here was peace and a clear conscience.

After Jesus' death, the sacred holy of holies in the temple was opened, the heavy veil that separated it from the people was torn from the top to the bottom by the hand of God. He asks us to come directly to him through Jesus. Forget the high priest. He is no longer necessary. Jesus is the only High Priest we need.

In a natural sense, we scrub and sanitize when we cut up a whole chicken or trim a roast to disinfect any areas blood might have contaminated. But Christ's blood offers a cleansing of the greatest degree! When I asked Christ into my heart, his blood figuratively washed away my sins. All of them.

A dear family friend died a few years ago. I can still hear his prayer: "We thank you for you, Jesus." I am challenged. Do I thank Jesus for the gift of himself?

prayer

Christ, I thank you for being the perfect sacrifice for my sins. Thank you for the blood that washes my soul. Help me daily remember to walk in your cleansing power.

reflection

Have you thanked God for the privilege of coming directly to him, without a high priest for an advocate? Most of all, thank God for sending Jesus to be the supreme sacrifice.

2

SACRIFICE OF OBEDIENCE

Hebrews 10

In the Old Testament, under the old law, God delighted to see the people offering sacrifices on an actual altar as a sign of their obedience. When Jesus, the sinless Lamb of God, died, God abolished the old law and established a new covenant. In today's Scripture text, we see what God really wants. Our hearts, our lives, our all.

In one sense, offering a literal animal was easier than offering God everything. I tend to hold on to cherished ideas, personality quirks, pet sins. Some things are hard to relinquish, but God wants it all, every bit. The Old Testament offerings had to be perfect. Today, God says, "Give me your hidden faults even if they are gross, ugly, and defiled. I redeemed you by the blood of Christ. You are mine."

When I accept Jesus' sacrifice and allow his blood to cleanse my heart from its sin stains and emptiness, he accepts me. He says, "I don't need those offerings any more. Better than any animal is your own self." I too must be crucified—to self and sin. I wish it were a once and done thing, but it's a little like dishes, laundry, or the house. You have to keep cleaning. It won't stay clean. Someday, in heaven, when God replaces our human bodies for eternal ones, we will be forever clean.

Obedience is far better than any animal sacrifice. I think of several families who have demonstrated practical obedience. Families who have left a known environment and culture to seek a more godly way. Those who have forsaken a comfortable lifestyle to pursue one filled with hardship and danger on a lonely mission field. People who have stepped away from their earthly families to follow God.

Does the sacrifice of obedience cost us? Absolutely. God never promised a painless giving of ourselves, but rather he promises he will be with us and that he delights in our sacrifices. No sacrifice goes unnoticed. He cares about all we give up, and he always replaces it with something better.

For a family who stepped out of a comfortable lifestyle to join a simpler, quieter way of life, he might give a community of friends. I know families who left the churches of their childhood to join churches they felt were more spiritual. They lost the friends of their youth but gained many brothers and sisters in Christ.

Families on the mission field know the completeness of surrender, and their sacrifice blesses many. Just one soul won for God is worth the sacrifice. Sometimes they might not know in this life how much their work has accomplished for God. But he knows.

Daily obedience to the Word is my sacrifice, which I must offer upon the altar of my will. Be it easy or tough, God notices. And he rewards me with peace and approval.

prayer

Lord, I give myself a sacrifice to you, knowing you delight in everything I give and honor my surrender. It's not easy, but it is completely worth it, because at the end of all the sacrifices, there is heaven.

reflection

What have you given up for God? Does it seem impossibly hard? Find someone who has also sacrificed much and tell them about your struggles. We often find encouragement in sharing.

3

HE WANTS BROKEN PIECES?

Psalm 51:1-17

Smash! Crash! The beautiful bowl, still holding half of the date pudding, landed on the floor. My small daughter pulled it off the counter, trying to help me put food away after the visitors had left. I sighed as I hunted for paper towels and a broom. Ruined. It was all ruined. The food and the bowl. Broken bits of glass mingled with the pudding, and I sent my daughter to another room to keep her safe. From broken glass and from my frustration.

But God loves broken things! I marvel at his plea to us: "Be broken! And then give me all the fragments." God wants broken bits? They are only worthy of the trash pile. He answers, "I will make something beautiful from the pieces."

My artist sister creates mosaics from broken bits of pottery. So I understand a little of how God can turn broken things into pieces of beauty. He is the master artist. The broken pieces of our lives, presented to him, represent humility and surrender, both of which are beautiful to our God.

In Isaiah 57:15, God tells us he is high and lofty, that he inhabits eternity and is named Holy. Yet he lives with those who have a contrite and humble heart. He promises to revive the repentant heart. To breathe new life into those broken pieces.

This is a sacrifice that truly costs. To be broken means pain. But it is a sacrifice that reveals God is at work in my life. And he pays attention to the sacrifice. He lovingly reaches down and picks up my shattered offering and tenderly comforts as he mends, soothes as he heals.

The patched pieces might show scars of healing, but that too is beautiful to God. Those who have been broken can offer encouragement to others who are struggling, unwilling to yield the pieces to the Master, the Healer, the Mender of all that is shattered.

Have you ever glued a china cup, only to discover a small piece is missing? That missing tiny chip spoils the entire cup. So it is with my heart. If I keep anything back in my heart of hearts for myself, it mars the beauty and usefulness of myself for God.

My friend said the first time her husband looked over their property with interest in buying, she hated the rocks. "That's all it is, Frank. A pile of rocks!" But she surrendered her dreams of lush farmland to submit to God's plan. Now those rocks are the focal point of her splendid garden that I wrote about in another meditation. Flowers grow up and around the rocks, flourishing to soften the hard edges of the boulders. The rocks speak of the mighty hand of God. She said, "What I most hated I now love most."

God does that. He turns the very thing that makes me cringe into a blessing and a beauty. But he has to have all the pieces of every broken heart, every hated bit. He appreciates and blesses a willing sacrifice.

prayer

Master Artist, healer of my heart, I give you all the broken dreams and the shattered pieces of my life. I know in your hands you can make them a beautiful blessing.

reflection

Does your life seem to lie in shatters around you? Pick up the pieces and give them to God. Above all, surrender your heart in humility to the One who mends it perfectly.

4

BE A LIVING
SACRIFICE

1 Peter 2:1-9; Romans 12:1

I've heard a story of a missionary who preached about giving everything to God. His listeners were poor but sincere. When the offering was taken, one man put the basket on the floor and stepped into it. He had only himself to give. But it was enough.

That's what God wants—my body, not slain as the animals on Old Testament altars, but alive and vibrant through his life in me, and eager to do God's will.

I give my hands to God. I enjoy art; does my work glorify God? I like to write letters; do they edify and encourage? I love to sing; do my songs praise my Maker? I cook, clean, stitch, plant, wash; can I do these tasks for his glory so they are acceptable to him?

My sister keeps charge of the details of my parents' lives: the doctor appointments and some of their medical needs. She arranges her schedule to take care of them, often dropping her own work to check in on Dad and Mom or to drive them someplace. And even more noteworthy—she does the lowly, menial duties that are hard for them, like trimming their toenails. All of these things are sacrifices, yet she willing gives her time to honor our parents, and therefore honors God. Her hands truly are God's.

My artist sister joyfully creates many items that she gives to others. Another grows gorgeous flowers and passes them out generously. Yet another sews clothes for gifts even though sewing isn't her favorite task. All of them are willing to listen when I am burdened. They are giving their talents to God as a part of the living sacrifice he requires.

My feet are God's. I ask him where to walk and when. He is faithful to guide, if I am faithful to seek his guidance. My mind is his. If I surrender it to him, he will keep my thoughts pure and honest. I appreciate a friend who is much more intelligent than I who kindly shares her expertise with me when I run into problems with a typing process or word error. This is using her mind to glorify God.

My time is God's. If I give it to him as a sacrifice, it won't be such a bother to me when my schedule is interrupted or rearranged. I admire the sacrifice a friend makes to daily drive her son to his workshop. It takes several hours from her day, yet I have never heard one word of complaint.

As a living sacrifice, I am joyfully God's. The ending of Romans 12:1 is always a challenge: ". . . which is your reasonable service." It's only reasonable for me to give my body to God. He has sacrificed so much for me—my body, my life, my heart, and my all are still only tiny sacrifices in comparison. Yet he loves me and accepts my pitiful little offering. He pays attention to what I do with this body. May it ever be in his will.

prayer

Lord, it's not much, this body. But it's all I have. And I give it to you. Use it for your glory.

reflection

Have you ever consciously given your body to God? Do so today. And every day glorify him in word, thought, and deed.

5

DOES IT COST TO PRAISE?

Psalm 116

*I*n my King James Bible, David's Psalm 116 is titled "Vows for Deliverance from Peril." It is full of pathos, strewn with trouble, sorrow, and even death. It may have been penned or sung as David hid from his enemies, his life in danger both day and night.

Yet he says, "I will offer to thee the sacrifice of thanksgiving" (verse 17). Didn't it cost David tremendously to speak this affirmation? It must have. Wouldn't it have been a lot easier to grumble, fret, moan, and weep? Those would be responses I could understand.

A dear friend lost her husband of nearly fifty-six years. Many of those years they were together 24/7. They fit each other like salt and pepper, like left and right shoes. He was the rock to her sunshine, the stabilizer behind her effervescence. I wondered how she would manage without him. But the grace of God is evident. Each time I talk to her she says, "I miss my husband, especially on birthdays, our anniversary, or other special days. But I am so glad we had those years together. I have so much to be thankful for." Never have I detected anger or bitterness even while she faces lonely days. She is offering the sacrifice of praise.

My aunt is facing a trial of cancer, that dreaded monster, with small hope of a cure unless God performs a miracle. She lost her husband five years ago, after watching him suffer with a lung disease. She too faces life—and death—with joy. This sacrifice of praise touches me deeply. How much more does the Father delight in it?

Another friend suffers with back pain. Yet she smiles bravely and refuses to complain about her pain. She does not like to even discuss her back, but she has to stand most of the time to deal with the pain. Instead of complaining she blesses others by focusing on God's love.

Someone said, "The world is full of grumpy people. Be a smiler." I was reminded of that when I stopped at an airline office to check on lost luggage. A worker said, astonished, "You're not upset." Why should I be? It's just "stuff." My joy is in God.

Does it cost to praise God? Absolutely. It costs my giving to and serving of others when I would prefer being served. It costs a surrender to all I hold dear. It costs a giving up of my "right" to complain when times are hard. It costs my will, which is the hardest thing of all to surrender.

Is the cost worth it? According to Jeremiah 33, God notices my sacrifice and honors my praise. "It shall be to me a name of joy . . . there shall be heard . . . the voice of them . . . that shall bring the sacrifice of praise into the house of the Lord" (verses 9-12). Verbally praising him is one of the best testimonies I can give to the world, to my friends, to my family. I am grateful whenever praise to God is mentioned in our biweekly prayer meeting.

"I will praise the name of God with a song, and will magnify him with thanksgiving. This also shall please the Lord better than an ox or bullock" (Psalm 69:30-31). May my prayers be not only requests, but also filled with the sacrifice of thanksgiving to God.

prayer

Father, I offer to you the sacrifice of praise and thanksgiving, for you are worthy. Teach me to surrender even my difficulties to you and to rejoice in your love.

reflection

Does life seem too tough for you to be joyful? Realize it's a sacrifice, a conscious effort to honor your Savior in praise. Offer it in humility and love.

6

FORGET THE SACRIFICE, GIVE MERCY

Micah 6:1-8

I have researched a little of the many sacrifices God required in the Old Testament. Now Christ is our sacrifice and we no longer have to make literal burnt offerings to him.

Jesus said, "I will have mercy, and not sacrifice" (Matthew 9:13). We know sacrifices are very important to God, so why does he now focus on mercy? In the same verse, Jesus says he didn't come to save the righteous—the ones who meticulously kept the law—but sinners: those who knew they messed up and needed a Savior.

After I have brought him my life, my soul, my heart, my mind, and my body as a living sacrifice, what then? Deuteronomy 10:12-13 is a companion Scripture to Micah 6:8: "What doth the Lord thy God require of thee, but to fear the Lord thy God, to walk in all his ways, and to love him, and to serve the Lord thy God with all thy heart and with all thy soul, To keep the commandments of the Lord . . . which I command thee this day for thy good?"

God's commands are made for my good, for the benefit of my soul. And they aren't impossible for me to perform. In Matthew 25, Jesus lists many things I can do to express my love for him. Visit the sick and the imprisoned, feed the hungry, give water to the thirsty, provide housing and clothing for the poor.

Does mercy cost? Absolutely. It costs time, money, energy. But mercy is only a reasonable response to the God of all mercy. Consider the nature of mercy: it is immeasurable, boundless, and free. It is mercy that sent Jesus to redeem me, mercy that sent the Holy Spirit to guide my steps, mercy that keeps calling me to come closer to him. His mercy is the motivation for my life.

Mercy has also been shown to me by others. My family forgives me when I become uptight about a deadline. My church family shows mercy when I overstep my duties and start organizing their lives. My friends are merciful when I am late with a card or phone call. God grant that I may never abuse this mercy and go carelessly or recklessly through life expecting them to forgive me. It is better when mercy jolts me to a stronger awareness of my faults so that I take pains to correct them.

I long to extend the same mercy to others instead of holding them to an impossibly high standard, which is a weakness of mine. I somehow expect them to conquer my own defeats. But by opening my heart to accept the mercy of God, I can learn to show mercy to the people in my life.

prayer

Heavenly Father, you are merciful far beyond what I deserve. Instead of sacrifice, today I bring a heart softened by your mercy, and one longing to share that mercy with others. Teach me to forgive and love, over and over.

reflection

Are you frustrated by your own weaknesses or those of others? Can you show mercy today, remembering how much mercy God showed you?

7

COMMUNICATE SACRIFICIALLY

Hebrews 13:10-21

I often ponder the words in Hebrews 13:16: "But to do good and to communicate, forget not: for with such sacrifices God is well pleased."

I know it takes a sacrifice to do good. It involves noticing needs and reaching out to alleviate pain. It includes acts of kindness, time spent in prayer, and words of affirmation.

Does communication require sacrifice? Think of it this way. My words and facial expressions convey a message. They too involve stepping out of my own safe cocoon of quietness to reach out to another. It includes becoming vulnerable, for someone may not agree with my ideas and plans. It takes humility to speak just as it takes humility to keep silent.

A sister-in-Christ listens without judging when I have a burden. She reminds me to give the problem to God and to refrain from gossiping to others about an issue. She also surrenders her will to her husband in a way that encourages me to follow Christ's teaching. "I will ask him," she says, before making a rash decision. "Did you talk to your husband?" she asks me. It cannot always be easy to direct others, but she does it for the glory of God.

When I was younger I envied people who were shy. I wondered how it would be to never need to apologize for talking too much. Wouldn't it be nice to be content to sit in a corner and listen? But being unwilling to talk can be ungracious. My mother taught me to graciously greet visitors at church and at home. My cousin, a quieter soul, often stood beside me at church and eventually joined me in conversation with a visitor. The first time I saw her walk up to a visitor all by herself, I rejoiced. She had learned to communicate to make a friend.

While I still must learn to control my speech, to listen sincerely instead of thinking of what I will say next, to focus more on others and a lot less about myself, I have learned it takes unselfishness to open my heart. Refusing to talk isn't something to envy but to pity. Communication involves interaction by all parties. Even a talkative person like me needs feedback for any conversation to continue. So just as I must learn when to be quiet, an introverted person should cultivate a willingness to share.

Transparency isn't easy. Interestingly, sometimes I find it easier to share personal struggles and victories with people I don't know well than with those with whom I live. Is it because I assume the ones who know me well will judge me by what I do, not by my heart? They might be thinking, "She says she loves God, but I just heard her slam the door in frustration."

The temptation to shut away my heart is real. Even writing can be an escape from reality. I must learn to be honest, penning not only the good and ideal, but also the human and faltering. It is a cost of communication that has heartfelt payoffs. I am rewarded by true friendships, honest encouragements, and unconditional love.

I am blessed by parents who demonstrated the sacrifice of communication. I have precious memories of popping into the study to tell my father about my day. He always made me feel as if I was just who he wanted to see. Mother also would drop her quilting while I cried to her about some struggle I faced.

In all the busyness of life, I must not forget to communicate: to share those words of love, to tell my neighbors of Jesus, to speak words of affirmation to my children, to shower my friends with grace in listening and in talking.

prayer

Lord, you have communicated your love in so many clear, touching ways. Teach me to reach out in honesty and love, my heart ever willing to speak and to listen.

reflection

Are you a talker or a listener? How can you build up your weaknesses to communicate in a way that shows God is strong in you?

1

EVEN THE DESERT MAY BLOOM

Isaiah 35

Here in the Northern California foothills, the climate is Mediterranean—rainy winters and warm, dry summers. At the end of the summer the air is so dry that some of us suffer from nosebleeds and flaky skin. The ground is dusty, with crackling leaves falling, and the only green things growing are where we water extensively.

Eagerly, we wait for the fall rains. The first raindrop is hailed with delight and thanksgiving to God. Soon more rain falls and green shoots spring up from the refreshed earth. In a few months the landscape is transformed and blossoming.

I see parallels to our spiritual lives. Some days I may feel dry, barren, and ugly. I see no obvious fruit, and my spirits wither. What could be the reason for this "desert"?

Sometimes it is sin. Sometimes it's simply a failure to keep our personal relationship with God vibrant and alive. I must pray even—or especially—when I don't feel like it. Sometimes it might be boredom with daily life. The soul faces seasons too. Hormones can affect my mood; stress of an overly full schedule might get my spirits down.

God has answers for everything I face and water for my desert. Once, when we had company back-to-back for weeks, I was weary of washing linens and cooking big meals. God led me to study one of Jesus' most stressful days.

According to Matthew 14, these things happened on one day: John the Baptist, Jesus' close friend and torchbearer, was beheaded.

When Jesus heard of it, he went by boat to grieve privately. People followed him, and in his great love and unselfishness, he ministered to them. Later the disciples wanted to send the people away, but Jesus fed them, using five loaves and two fishes as the beginning of a feast. Surely his day was full enough! But no—his disciples were on the sea heading back home when a storm sprang up.

Jesus had sent everyone away and had finally found time alone to pray. But now his love again moved him. He walked across the battering waves and brought a miracle to Peter and the other disciples. Reading this chapter changed my attitude so completely that I was able to keep serving joyfully.

This has challenged me to read the Bible earnestly. It is good to ask God for "showers of blessing" (Ezekiel 34:26). There is no reason for my soul to shrivel for lack of heavenly rain, because God's storehouse of blessing is available always, everywhere. God longs to water my soul with his love, grace, and blessings. Even when things don't go as I wish, my spirit can rejoice because I am redeemed by the blood of Christ. Praise God—my soul will blossom as the rose!

prayer

Dear Lord, you are the giver of the water that saves my soul. You know what it is to be exhausted and yet to keep on going. Help me never to stay in the desert, but to seek out the water of your Word that will nourish even my driest days.

reflection

Do you feel dry and withered? How can you drink from God's living water today?

2

NO WATER, NO LIFE

Psalm 63

Before we moved to California, we checked out various locations. Some men, including my husband, scouted a radius of about one hundred miles, eventually settling on the foothills of the Sierra Nevada in Northern California.

We found the locals generally pleasant and welcoming. The land abounded with natural resources, and we were exultant over the citrus fruits available. One thing no one mentioned was water. We didn't think to inquire, "Are the wells sufficient? Is the water pure and abundant?"

So we moved there. We hired a driller to dig a well. A long, anxious day ended with the auger deep in 780 feet of rock, soil, clay, limestone. But no water. The well driller chose another probable spot, and the next day he drilled 320 feet. No water.

We were stunned. We had prayed about this. Didn't God care? What good were fifty acres of land if we had no water to nourish growth? There was no city water available. We couldn't afford to drill another well.

The driller folded up his equipment and went home. Discouraged and nearly out of money, we told our neighbor, from whom we had bought the property. He said, "We have lots of water, but I know there are others who don't. This area is a little sparse in good wells."

Our first thought was, "Now you tell us!" He kindly offered the use of his well. We had few choices, so we accepted his generous offer. My husband bought a tank that fit onto a small trailer, and every few days he went to the neighbor's to fill the tank from a garden hose.

We became water policemen. If someone showered too long, the ones waiting would yell, "I want to bathe too!" We used our dishwater for many things: to clean vehicles and footwear, to water a few plants. I was amazed how long the tank lasted for our family, which at that time numbered six. We were living temporarily in a travel trailer while we built our house, so we did use less water than we would in a large house.

I sought verses that assured me of God's provision and care. The story of the thirsty Israelites in Exodus 17 was encouraging. God told Moses to strike a rock, and water flowed out. Enough for the thousands! If he could do that, he would provide for us too.

He still promises water. Living water! If we drink of him and immerse ourselves in his Word, he will give to us "a well of water springing up into everlasting life" (John 4:14).

prayer

Creator of living water, thank you for providing for our needs when we didn't know where to find water. Thank you most of all for the water of life.

reflection

Do you have plenty of water? Have you thanked God for this essential gift of life?

3

LIFE THAT'S MORE ABUNDANT

John 10:1-11

*W*ater is important! Without it we would die. We can live longer without food than without water. Water is totally God-made. Humans cannot duplicate God's wonderful life-giving water! They may add flavor, sweetener, carbonation, or caffeine, but the original liquid is still God's creation.

Those first years after we moved to California, we were very aware of how essential water is. God turned our dry wells into blessing. For a long time we borrowed water from the neighbor's well. This became a period of becoming friends and of sharing our faith.

One day my husband was delighted to see that one dry well was producing a little water. We pumped it into a holding tank, and from there into our now-completed house. It was sufficient for basic needs, but when we planted a garden and a lawn, we were quick to discover that we needed a lot more water than the half gallon a minute that well gave.

It wasn't always easy, but we committed our problem to the One who controls and creates all the water in the world. As we waited on God to show us his plan, we found that although the land could be nearly dry physically, we could still be flourishing spiritually. He gave us grace to rejoice and to find victory over the discouragement that threatened to overwhelm us.

Two years after our move we were able to dig yet another well. My husband prayed that morning, "Lord, you know our needs. Six gallons of water per minute would be sufficient to fill our needs. We trust in you."

We let family and friends know that the well driller was here again. They joined us in prayer. God answered those prayers above and beyond anything we could imagine. Shortly after noon I went to see how it was going. The driller looked at me with awe. He said, "You have an artesian well! It pumps more than thirty gallons of water a minute, and bubbles out of the top at a rate of five gallons a minute."

"We prayed for this well," I answered, tears pushing at my eyes. We were completely overwhelmed by God's answer. It is now years later, but still, often when we pass the well, my husband and I will look at each other, marveling, "God is so good!"

Spiritually, he also wants us to experience more than enough. There's not much blessing in just getting by when God promises abundant life. Life that grows and flourishes will multiply to minister and bless others. Life that is victorious over sin will encourage others, and life that is vibrant and joyful will always be an inspiration.

prayer

Lord, you have showed us a miracle of natural water. Just as it is above and beyond our expectations, so may my spiritual life grow with your abundance.

reflection

Are you just barely getting by spiritually? What will you do to find God's abundant life?

4

WATER FOR MY SOUL

Isaiah 41:10-20

*I*n the fall of 1996, my husband and I, with our two little ones, were asked to move to Beckwourth, California, to join a mission outreach. We had never dreamed of living out West, but for two years? That seemed possible, doable. Neither did we imagine that California would become home and grab us deeply as it did. Those two years changed our lives.

About a year after we moved, we were very homesick. A few disagreements had arisen at our tiny church, and although we were becoming fast friends with our new church family, back in Missouri everyone went about their own work, gatherings, birthday celebrations, and church functions, and we missed that! The distance seemed to loom like a shadow that darkened each day.

One day, in the midst of our homesickness, we received a letter from a cousin. He is not a letter writer—that was the only time we ever heard from him. But the simple words of encouragement and the Bible verses he penned moved us deeply. We wept and then cheered up. By God's grace, and through the prayers of those we loved, we could go on! Never again did homesickness threaten to derail us. We were able to work through the situations that looked so disagreeable.

That letter was a messenger of hope, as it says in Proverbs 25:25: "As cold waters to a thirsty soul, so is good news from a far country." God knows just how much we need that good news and when it will encourage us the most.

Another amazing answer to a heart's need came at a time when my husband and I were both struggling spiritually. He had been troubled about sins from his boyhood, and I was facing postpartum depression. We prayed and prayed. Sunday morning, we sat at church, both heavy of heart and unbelievably sad.

When the minister stood up to preach, he said that he didn't know exactly what God had in mind, but that the sermon had been changed twice. Earlier in the week he had chosen a subject, and later he felt he should change it. Then just this morning, sitting at church, he felt a heavy burden. He strongly felt that God had still a different message he wanted his servant to preach. When he started sharing what God had laid on his heart, I burst into tears. Cleansing tears. This message was exactly what we had prayed for! Forgiveness, assurance of God's love. His grace and strength filled our hearts and showed us the steps we both needed to gain victory.

No one else may have needed that sermon, but knowing that God pours out his waters of mercy to even just two people who need it most was an amazing faith booster.

God daily shows us his love. When life seems a desert, unfruitful and ugly, God sends a word, a message, a flower to show us that he is our oasis. His streams of water never run dry. "His compassions fail not. They are new every morning: great is thy faithfulness" (Lamentations 3:22–23).

prayer

Thank you, Lord, for giving me glimpses of your life-giving water when I feel barren and unfruitful. Teach me to find my oasis in your love.

reflection

Do you wonder if God cares for you personally? Find something that he has done for you this week. Tell someone about it.

5

UNLIMITED BY DROUGHT

Psalm 1

*P*hysically, we need water for life and sustenance. In California, the "water wars" continue each year. Do the farmers deserve more water than the large cities? Who gets priority?

Most of the state's water comes from the northern areas, but the majority of the people live in the south. They are dependent upon the rain and snow that falls in the Sierras. Northern companies with reservoirs can charge high premiums for their water and may even decide who gets the most.

Cities regulate water use and encourage us to tear out lawns. We can replace them with rocks or, at the very least, plant drought-tolerant shrubs and trees if we insist on something green. Wherever we turn, we see suggestions for lessening water usage.

When we are lavishly watering our lawn, and our gardens and flowers flourish, we may find a water policeman knocking at our door. In the cities, people face fines for excessive water usage. We want to be prudent in water use and thank God for providing an abundance of water on our farm.

Could I be chided for being lavish in kindness? Might I even be accused of being too fruitful, perhaps for helping someone too much, or for being too forgiving? But God will never chastise me for being too fruitful. He longs for me to be growing more and more.

God's Word encourages—no—*commands* me to grow and flourish like a well-watered garden. He doesn't want me to only grow cacti, Bermuda grass, or rocks. He longs to see my life

flourishing and reaching out to bless others. He wants my life to
bring forth something beautiful.

As a dry land soaks up any rain that falls, so I long for God's
water. That sparkling, nourishing, refreshing water of the Word.
If I thirst after it, he will fill my life to overflowing. He always
promises to supply more than I need. And when my life sends out
branches that provide shade or fruit for the hungry, may I recognize
that it is only through God and his water that I have anything at all
to share.

prayer

Lord, in a dry and thirsty land,
I know where the source of true
water lies: in you! Show me how
to let your water nourish and fill
me so that I am overflowing with
your graces.

reflection

How might you be like a tree that
flourishes because of being planted beside a river?

6

I'LL NEVER THIRST?

John 4:6-30

Once when we drove "the loneliest road in America," Highway 50 across Nevada, we stopped for fuel in a town one hundred miles from any other. Our water supply was depleted, so I went to a sandwich shop and asked for "the biggest water cup you have." The clerk didn't blink or smile. He just reached down and gave me an enormous glass, possibly half of a gallon, and I started gulping it greedily. Ah, what a lifesaver!

Before my father-in-law knew he had diabetes, he was also very thirsty. He couldn't seem to drink anything that quenched his thirst for longer than a few minutes. When he mentioned it to a friend, he was told to see a doctor. Yes, it was diabetes.

A constant thirst may indicate that something is wrong physically. But in a spiritual sense, I should never lose my thirst for God's Word.

I try to imagine being with the woman at the well the day she met Jesus. She knew what it was to be thirsty. Going to the well for water was a daily duty. Now Jesus told her that he had living water for her. Living water? How could water be alive?

She must have been puzzled; she asked him how he planned to get the water, because she saw he didn't even have a pail. But Jesus must have just smiled kindly. He sensed that her heart was thirsty too.

"You have water that will make me never thirst again?" She did not know how that was possible, and yet, oh how wonderful it would be if she could quit coming to the well for water.

I love the way that Jesus tells her that he would give her this water if she asks for it. He still wants me to ask for that living water.

It is water that saves my soul, water that makes my whole life new and glorious.

She didn't really understand how it could be that Jesus' water would be a well of everlasting life within her, but she understood enough to run and tell others about it. Neither can I explain all that I experience when Jesus fills me with his living water, but I too want to tell others about the source of living water.

It seems like a paradox: to continually thirst after him and yet to be filled with his water so that I will never thirst again. The thirst that I will not face again is a thirst for fulfillment, a hunger for something more. God has created all of us with a vacuum that he alone can fill. That's the thirst he promises to quench. Best of all, my life can be a well that springs into everlasting life. That's the life I want!

prayer

Thank you, Lord, for your promise of everlasting water, everlasting life. May my life be filled with your water and overflow to others.

reflection

Do you thirst after God? What will you do today to satiate that longing?

7

HEAVEN'S RIVER
OF LIFE

Revelation 21:3-6; 22:1-6

*W*henever it rained, my sister's well produced muddy water. No matter how thirsty she and her family were, they couldn't possibly drink the well water. It was no fun to haul water home when the well was right there, but who would risk disease by drinking dirty water?

Until the well was cleaned and had a new lining installed, they hauled water in. My sister thought she wouldn't take clear, sparkling water for granted again.

In Missouri we had a good supply of water, but it was sulfur water. No matter how hard we tried, we simply couldn't get used to that rotten-egg smell. We finally purchased a whole-house purifying system. Once we did that, the water was delicious.

In Exodus 15, the children of Israel were in the desert and water wasn't abundant. On this day they came to some water and were very excited, until they discovered that the water was bitter. Then they were discouraged and complained loudly to Moses. As usual, Moses took this burden to God. The Lord showed Moses a piece of wood and told him to throw it into the water. Immediately the water became sweet.

God often uses many things as illustrations of something more, something deeper. In this instance, he said that if they would always diligently listen to and obey his voice, he would keep them from getting the diseases that plagued the Egyptians.

Wouldn't I like to locate that tree? To think of always having a supply of perfect, life-giving water and, best of all, to never get sick again—that would be amazing.

God promises all of that to me. In Revelation 21, he promises that if I thirst after him, he will give me water from the fountain of life. Not just a stingy trickle. But freely. I can picture a splashing fountain; water that sparkles in the sunlight, water that overflows with glorious abundance.

The angel of heaven next showed John water that was as clear as crystal—the river of life. Beside this wondrous river grew a tree that was simply incredible. It bore twelve fruits, one kind per month.

We once saw a tree that had been grafted to bear fourteen fruits. Somehow I don't think that God's tree of life took any grafting or years of experiments. He is God. He is life. And may we someday be gathered by the river of life, eating joyfully of the fruit of the tree of life!

prayer

Thank you, Lord, for providing a source of pure water, both now and in eternity.

reflection

Are you filled with God's pure water? Think about the river of life and thank him.

FAQS ABOUT PLAIN MENNONITES

The Author Answers

1. WHAT IS A MENNONITE? HOW DO YOU DIFFER FROM AMISH?

In Switzerland in the 1500s, a new group of Christians was interested in reforming the Roman Catholic Church. These Christians desired to follow the Bible more completely. They were called "Anabaptists" because they rejected infant baptism and embraced what they called believers baptism (Mark 16:16). The Anabaptists were persecuted, and many were killed because the Roman Catholic Church thought this new belief was heretical.

Menno Simons was one of the leaders who left the Catholic priesthood to follow Christ. The name "Mennonite" comes from his name. Jacob Ammon helped the group that later was called Amish. In fundamental beliefs, various Amish groups are very similar to Mennonites, although our particular Mennonite group, called Fellowship Churches, is more progressive than some Amish. We have electricity and telephones in our houses and we drive vehicles.

Mennonites believe the Bible is the inspired Word of God, and we try to follow it as our guide for daily life. We believe all are lost without Christ and that salvation is only through the blood of Jesus.

Some fundamentals are teachings on moral purity (Mark 10:2-12), nonresistance (Matthew 5:39, 44), obedience to civil laws (Romans 13:1-7), separation from the world (2 Corinthians 6:14-17; 2 John 2:15-17), and evangelism (Mark 16:15).

2. WHY DO THE WOMEN AND GIRLS WEAR THOSE HATS?

We take the teaching in 1 Corinthians 11:1-16 literally. Women cover their uncut hair with a covering or prayer veiling. This also shows we accept God's order of headship. Distinctive attire between men and women, as well as distinctive roles, are included here. Our girls start wearing the prayer covering at age four, when their understanding of the Biblical teaching is growing.

3. ARE WOMEN PUSHED BACK OR TRAMPLED ON?

Not at all. We are one in Christ (Galatians 3:28); while women are commanded to submit to their husbands (Ephesians 5:22-24), the husbands are also commanded to love their wives and treat them with deference (1 Peter 3:7). It involves a sharing of ideas and lives; it's a relationship of equals with differing roles. Women do not formally teach men, but they do informally teach each other (1 Timothy 2:9-12; Titus 2:3-5).

4. WHAT KIND OF EDUCATION DO YOUR CHILDREN RECEIVE?

We use an intense curriculum that requires study and diligent application. After eight years of formal schooling, most of the graduates test at twelfth grade or higher in California achievement tests. State laws do not have requirements for private schools as they do for public schools. Some people have taken the GED test, and some have gotten high school diplomas, especially if they need them for a job. Others have taken education courses by mail. In general, we have been able to find work that doesn't require more than the eighth-grade education, such as farming, carpentry, auto mechanic work, and furniture building.

5. DON'T YOU GET BORED WITH YOUR QUIET LIVES?

This question is sometimes asked when people hear we don't have television or go to the movies, races, or amusement parks. Our lives are full and blessed, with Christ as our fulfillment. But we also know God wants his children to be refreshed physically and mentally in wholesome recreation. We sing, play games as a family, and read a lot, and occasionally the youth from church spend an evening together in recreation and fellowship. They also enjoy an annual "youth day," sometimes with youth from another congregation.

We also enjoy traveling to see God's creation. The Pacific coast is one of our favorite destinations.

6. CAN OTHER PEOPLE COME TO YOUR CHURCH?

Anyone is welcome to attend our church and also to become a member. Mennonites aren't a particular ethnic group, and members from our church come from various backgrounds. We welcome questions and try to openly share our faith and practice.

ABOUT THE AUTHOR

Faith Sommers is a conservative Mennonite mother, wife, and columnist for *Ladies Journal*, a publication for Amish and Mennonite women. She (center, back row) and her husband Paul live in California and are pictured here with their six children, born to them between 1994 and 2007.